Mo~~~

Home

The home care worker's guide to handling
other people's finances and belongings

Money At Home

The home care worker's guide to handling
other people's finances and belongings

Pauline Thompson

BOOKS

Dedication

This book was the inspiration of Evelyn McEwen, Director of Information at Age Concern England, who sadly died before publication. She was a true champion of older people who, whilst engaged in broad policy issues, never forgot the importance of the practical details. This book is dedicated to her memory in the hope that it reflects her intentions and her spirit.

©2003 Age Concern England
Published by Age Concern England
1268 London Road
London SW16 4ER

First published 2003

Editor Sue Henning
Production Vinnette Marshall and Sue Henning
Design and typesetting GreenGate Publishing Services
Printed in Great Britain by Bell & Bain Ltd, Glasgow

A catalogue record for this book is available from the British Library

ISBN 0-86242-293-0

Bulk orders
Age Concern England is pleased to offer customised editions of all its titles to UK companies, institutions or other organisations wishing to make a bulk purchase. For further information, please contact the Publishing Department at the address on this page. Tel: 020 8765 7200. Fax: 020 8765 7211. Email: books@ace.org.uk

Contents

About the author

Pauline Thompson is the Policy Officer for Community Care (Finance) at Age Concern England. Prior to this, she worked for many years in local authorities as a social worker, latterly working with people with learning disabilities and involved in setting up group homes for people leaving hospital. This experience led to an interest in benefits and ensuring that service users got all the benefits to which they were entitled. For the last 10 years before coming to Age Concern, she worked as a Welfare Rights Officer and provided training in benefits. She was also a member of the Local Government Association's Social Security Advisers Group and took the lead on issues related to benefits and charging. She is a co-author of CPAG's *Paying for Care Handbook*, and the Disability Alliance's *Disability Rights Handbook*. She has a wealth of experience in the practical issues concerning handling service users' money.

Acknowledgements

For a variety of reasons, this book has taken a long time in preparation. My thanks to the many people I have contacted in the course of writing it to check out practice around the country. Particular thanks go to the advisory group who helped me scope out the book and who commented on the first draft: Doreen Field; June Hamilton-Hall; Christine Hawthorn; Brenda McKie; Geraldine Penfield; Mary Rutherford; Kate Telfer; Sue Todd; and Maggie Uttley. My thanks also to Stephen Boyo, Gretel Jones, Stephen Lowe and Sally West in the Age Concern Policy Unit who have helped me keep up with all the policy changes that have occurred whilst writing this book, and to Ginny Jenkins and Gary Fitzgerald of Action on Elder Abuse for their very helpful comments. Very grateful thanks to Leslie Bell, Director of Initiatives in Care Ltd and Chairperson of the Joint Advisory Group of Domiciliary Care Associations, and Peter Dunn from the Department of Health, who have been so helpful throughout, especially in the latter stages of its production. Last, but certainly not least, my heartfelt thanks go to Sue Henning for her patient editing of this book and bearing with the many last minute changes to keep it up to date. Any mistakes, of course, are entirely my own.

Introduction

In 1996, Age Concern Books published *Residents' Money*, a good practice guide, which looked at issues concerning the private finances of people living in residential care settings. *Money at Home* covers a larger and more diverse section of the population – those people, many of them older people, who live in their own homes but who have home care workers and volunteers to support them. It covers an important aspect of that support – the way that the financial matters of the person using the service (the service user) should be handled.

A wide range of organisations, agencies and individuals care for people living in their own homes and it is essential that those working with older people should understand the issues relating to handling a service user's money and belongings, especially if that person is physically or mentally frail.

Until the late 1980s and early 1990s, local authorities provided 'home help' services, which were largely concentrated on simple domestic tasks such as cleaning, shopping and collecting pensions and benefits. Now these tasks are more likely to be part of a much larger 'package of care', offering more intimate personal care such as help with washing and dressing. Often these services are no longer directly provided by the local authority, but have been arranged under contract with private or voluntary agencies. Nevertheless, the 'simple' practical services such as shopping and collecting pensions and benefits remain a vital part of the package of care that helps service users remain in their own home.

Often, local authorities have ceased to provide or arrange practical services, if that is all that is needed by the service user. Private or voluntary agencies or individuals directly employed by the service user have filled this gap.

The size of the home care service

The number of older people living at home seems set to increase, as more people are expected to live longer and, with support, remain in their own homes. This support will often include the need for paid carers or volunteers to help service users with their finances. This may be because a physical disability means that the person cannot get to the bank, or do their shopping. Or it may be because the person is no longer mentally capable of managing their financial affairs.

There are many thousands of carers – both paid and unpaid – who undertake a wide variety of tasks to help people stay in their own homes and live as independently as possible. In addition to the six million informal (sometimes called family) carers in the UK, the Department of Health estimates that there are 185,000 paid home care workers, employed by statutory, private or voluntary organisations. This figure does not include those who are employed directly by the individual, or those who visit as a volunteer through schemes run by local authorities or voluntary agencies. Nor does it include staff linked to sheltered housing schemes or nursing staff who visit older people.

The community care reforms and beyond

The thrust of the community care reforms in the late 1980s and early 1990s placed priority on the care of people in their own homes rather than in a care home. In the run-up to these reforms, the Government's White Paper, *Caring for People – Community Care in the Next Decade and Beyond* (1989), had as its first objective: 'to promote the development of domiciliary, day and respite services to enable people to live in their own homes wherever feasible and sensible'.

This commitment has continued and the Government's White Paper, *Modernising Social Services* (1998), states that services should 'enable adults assessed as needing social care support to live as safe, full and as normal life as possible, in their home wherever feasible'. The key principles in the paper include that:

- care should be provided to people in a way that supports their independence and respects their dignity;
- services should meet individual's specific needs, pulling together social services, health, housing, education and any other necessary support. People should have a say in what services they get and how they are delivered;

- every person – child or adult – should be safeguarded against abuse, neglect or poor treatment whilst receiving care;
- people who receive social services should have an assurance that the staff they deal with are sufficiently trained and skilled for the work they are doing. And staff themselves should feel included within a framework which recognises their commitment.

Although the trend since the community care reforms has been for local authorities to target help for those with high levels of need, more recently the Government has emphasised services which help people do things for themselves for as long as possible. Local authorities have been encouraged to develop rehabilitation and other support services designed to:

- enable people to live independently and to promote their social inclusion;
- enable people to exercise self-determination (and so make their own choices about where and how they live) and to live independently through lower levels of intervention.

The volume and complexity of the home care tasks seems set to continue. Within these tasks, the need for help with a wide range of financial matters will remain as important as ever, and perhaps increase as older people remain at home for longer.

The range of financial tasks

The wide range of tasks involving finance, which can be undertaken on an occasional or regular basis, includes:

- collecting pensions and benefits, if the person cannot get to the local post office or bank;
- shopping;
- helping with budgeting;
- collecting home care charges;
- watching out for financial abuse;
- dealing with money and financial affairs, when a person lacks capacity to manage;
- ensuring property and belongings are secure.

As well as handling money, home care workers can play a key role in informing the people they visit of the state benefits available or of new methods of shopping or banking, such as telephone or internet services, which could prove useful, especially if the person is housebound. Often, the home care worker is the first to pick up on the early signs of confusion about money matters or if a person is being financially abused.

Whenever money is handled for a service user, the home care worker is placed in a position of trust, even if it is just a one-off occasion. In the vast majority of cases, there are no problems but, even in the best relationships, misunderstandings can occur or the unexpected happen.

Improving care standards

The Care Standards Act 2000 has brought in provisions to regulate domiciliary care, as well as care in care homes. In this book, the term 'home care' is mainly used, although 'domiciliary care' is used in the National Minimum Standards. A National Care Standards Commission (NCSC) was set up in April 2002, and is the regulatory body that registers both care homes and home care agencies, which will have to meet the National Minimum Standards. It ensures that these standards, relating to the care of service users, are met by agencies providing personal care. It will also investigate any complaints against services that are registered. (It will be replaced by the Commission for Social Care Inspection during 2004. See page 134 for further details.)

The Care Standards Act 2000 also introduced a General Social Care Council (GSCC), which set codes of conduct and practice for staff and employers in the care professions, which they will have to sign up to. It will hold a general register of those staff, the purpose of which is to protect service users by preventing unsuitable people from being employed in the profession. The GSCC also regulates social work education and training.

A further body, which aims to improve the quality of social care, is the Social Care Institute for Excellence (SCIE). It will create a knowledge base of good practice in social care by sharing information on what works well, and produce good practice guidelines.

Regulation and guidance

Following the Care Standards Act 2000, from 1 April 2003 the home care market comes under regulation in the form of a registration scheme, which applies to all agencies providing personal domiciliary care, including local authorities. Some of the regulations and standards also apply to those employment agencies which act solely as introducers of home care workers who are directly employed by the service user (see Chapter 3). Registration under the regulations does not apply to individuals providing personal care on a self-employed or directly-employed basis; it only applies to agencies.

Personal care is defined in the Domiciliary Care National Minimum Standards (referred to throughout this book as the National Minimum Standards) as:

- assistance with bodily functions such as feeding, bathing and toileting;
- care falling just short of assistance with bodily functions, but still involving physical and intimate touching, including activities such as helping a person get out of a bath and helping them to get dressed;
- non-physical care, such as advice, encouragement and supervision relating to the foregoing, such as prompting a person to take a bath and supervising them during this;
- emotional and psychological support, including the promotion of social functioning, behaviour management, and assistance with cognitive functions.

It is the Department of Health's view that **only the first and second bullet points will give rise to registration as a home care agency**. The regulations do not apply to agencies that just provide domestic cleaning and other 'non-personal' services such as shopping or collecting pensions and benefits, or the type of personal care outlined above in bullet points three and four. However, it is up to the National Care Standards Commission to decide (taking into account the facts of a particular case and the law) whether or not the home care agency has to be registered.

The National Minimum Standards include the requirement to have policies and procedures in place to cover handling a service user's money and property, and responding to financial irregularities and abuse. The relevant standards for policies and procedures, financial protection, protection of the person, security of the home, confidentiality, autonomy and independence, record-keeping, records kept in the home, and financial procedures are reproduced in Appendix 1.

The National Minimum Standards identify a level of service below which an agency providing personal care must not fall. Although individuals and some agencies are not required to meet the standards, they might nevertheless provide useful guidelines.

Both the British Association of Domiciliary Care Officers (BADCO) and the United Kingdom Home Care Association (UKHCA) have produced good practice guides (see Appendix 4 for contact details).

Who is this book for?

This book is written primarily for home care workers, who handle money or deal with some aspects of their service user's financial affairs, and for managers, who are responsible for devising procedures on the handling of money. It will also be useful to staff and volunteers in any setting, who visit people in their own home in an official capacity, and who may be involved in assisting with some financial matters – social services departments, home care agencies, staff and managers in sheltered housing schemes, adult placement and group homes. People working in the health care professions may find certain sections particularly useful, as although they are unlikely to become involved in the day-to-day finances of a patient, they could find themselves being offered gifts or be concerned about a patient being financially abused.

The book will also be useful for home care workers who are self-employed or who are directly employed by the individual. Often working alone, they do not have the safeguards and structures of an agency policy behind them. Whilst some may have worked for agencies in the past and so be familiar with the types of procedures that exist, others need to be aware of the legal and financial implications of their actions, and not just rely on 'common sense'. Independent living groups, which are being set up to support service users who receive state payments through the Independent Living Fund or from direct payments from their local authority (see Chapter 3), will find it helpful to consider the issues raised in this book.

Although this book is written primarily for those working with older people – currently around 85 per cent of home care provided or arranged by local authorities is provided to older people – it will also be of use to those working with younger people, as many of the issues are the same.

Definition of 'home care worker' and 'service user'

The term 'home care worker' covers anyone who provides care or practical services in a professional or voluntary capacity to people (service users) in their own homes. This includes self-employed or directly-employed home care workers, as well as staff and volunteers in a local authority, or a voluntary or independent agency. It also covers housing and health staff who visit people in their own homes.

The term 'service user' covers anyone who receives care or practical services from the local authority, a voluntary or independent agency, a housing or health service, or from self-employed or directly-employed home care workers. It also includes 'informal' or 'family' carers who receive services in their own right under the Carers and Disabled Children Act 2000, or who employ a person to undertake tasks in their home in order that they can carry out their caring role.

There is a glossary of other terms used in this book on page 134.

How to use this book

This book is intended to be used mainly as a reference book. Readers can use the contents pages, index and cross-referencing in the text to find areas of key interest.

The book starts by covering general points about procedures for handling the finances and belongings of service users. It then looks at financial transactions – shopping, benefits, bills and banking – all situations when the home care worker may be handling money directly for the service user. It continues by covering areas of concern for home care workers who are self-employed or employed directly by the service user; information about benefits; what to do if the service user can no longer manage their own finances; security and insurance; gifts, wills and bequests; responding to financial abuse; and collecting charges from service users.

Throughout the book, case studies are used to illustrate the points made and to give good practice suggestions. Whilst many of the situations are based on actual events, the names have been changed to protect the individuals concerned. At the end of each chapter are *Do* and *Don't* lists that cover the key points to consider. The contact details for organisations mentioned in the text can be found in Appendix 4.

Please note *There are increasing differences in the law in England, Scotland, Wales and Northern Ireland. It is important to note that this book is written to reflect the law and practice in England. However, many aspects of law and guidance are similar across the UK, and the principles behind dealing with money and belongings should be the same. Readers in Wales, Scotland and Northern Ireland are strongly advised to check the current situation locally.*

Key principles when handling money or belongings

Most of us who are fit and able do not give a second thought to the importance of handling our own money. We decide where we want to shop and what we want to buy and only the lack of money may curb what we do – and not always then! Once we are no longer able to get to the shops, we lose the ability to make that snap decision to make a spontaneous purchase. We have lost some freedom of choice. If we need someone to collect our pensions and benefits, they will have a good idea of our level of income and perhaps our capital. We have lost some privacy. If we have become confused, someone may have to take over all control of our finances. We have lost aspects of both freedom of choice and privacy.

These are some basic principles that will be stressed throughout this book:

- the service user retains the right to choose and control how their money is spent, and should be encouraged and helped in this;
- there should always be the assumption that a person is capable of managing their financial affairs until they demonstrate otherwise;
- home care workers should not be involved unnecessarily in any aspect of an individual's financial affairs;
- confidentiality must be maintained when dealing with an individual's financial affairs;
- all home care workers should follow any laid-down procedures to safeguard themselves and the service user;
- home care workers should not gain in any way from undertaking financial transactions on behalf of service users.

1 Procedures

This chapter looks at the responsibilities of home care workers and managers in relation to procedures, and outlines the general considerations that need to be borne in mind when writing or altering them.

Procedures are important to protect both staff and service users. Home care workers care mainly for very vulnerable people, often alone, and they have to make decisions in response to particular situations. Procedures should set out the rules or expectations about how such situations will be handled. They should also help home care workers to be aware of, and clear about, the framework within which they work.

The National Minimum Standards (see Appendix 1) specify that registered home care agencies should have clear policies and procedures to support practice and meet the requirements of legislation. Those relevant to the issues in this book include: confidentiality of information; disclosure of abuse and bad practice; handling money and financial matters on behalf of a service user; maintaining the records in the home; acceptance of gifts and legacies; entering and leaving a service user's home; and safe keeping of keys.

Whilst self-employed or directly-employed home care workers are less likely to have any pre-agreed 'procedures', some of the more pertinent points could be incorporated into a written contract with a service user, to avoid misunderstandings. Someone employing a home care worker could also draw on the National Minimum Standards.

Responsibilities of home care workers

Home care workers should always remember that procedures have been developed as a safeguard to them, as well as to the service user. Those working for local authorities or independent agencies, which have written procedures about handling service users' finances, should always read them, discuss any queries with their home care manager, and then sign that they have understood them. Home care workers should keep their copy of the procedures in a safe, accessible place, where it can be found and checked, if necessary. If procedures about handling finances are not given at the time of appointment, home care workers should ask for a copy of their organisation's current procedures. From April 2003 it is a requirement under the National Minimum Standards that 'staff understand and have access to up-to-date copies of all policies, procedures and codes of practice'.

If home care workers find that some of the procedures are not helpful in their work, they should discuss these with their manager, who can make additions or revisions, if it is deemed necessary and after full consultation. Home care workers should always be consulted for their views when other circumstances arise that may require a change in procedures, to ensure that the procedures work on a day-to-day basis.

When procedures are revised, it is important for home care workers to destroy any out-of-date procedures to ensure that they are following the most recent version. Home care workers should sign that they have read and understood the revised procedures.

If a service user asks a home care worker to undertake a financial task that is not covered in the procedures, the home care worker should always check with their manager before undertaking such a task. Home care workers should not collude with service users and should raise any problems with their manager, particularly if the service user persistently wants the home care worker to flout the procedures.

Home care workers should be clear about which aspects of the procedures have to be followed at all times, with no deviation. They should also be aware that circumstances may arise when written permission, granted by their manager or another senior member of staff, might enable the procedures to be relaxed, providing the service user also agrees in writing. They can be helped in this through discussion with their managers and on-going training, as necessary.

Sometimes independent home care agencies provide a package of care, in which some of the care is provided under contract to the local authority and some bought from the agency directly by the service user. In such cases, the home care worker should make sure they are clear whether they follow the agency procedures or the local authority procedures.

Even if it is not expected that a home care worker (or other visitors such as district nurses, staff in sheltered housing schemes, and volunteers) would regularly handle a service user's finances, they should be aware of the procedures, as they may be asked or need to be involved occasionally: for example, they may be asked to undertake a task which involves handling the service user's money, as an emergency or on a temporary basis; they may be asked about financial matters; or they may be offered a gift.

General considerations for home care managers

Clear written procedures, as well as being a regulatory requirement for agencies providing personal care, are essential for the protection of the service user, staff and the organisation. They can help reduce the isolation of the home care workers so that they feel they are working within a structure and not having to make up the rules as they go along. Careful thought needs to be given to the whole process of writing procedures, how that information is imparted to staff and service users, and how the procedures are monitored.

Procedures on handling service users' finances need to dovetail with any conditions of service, codes of practice and any local procedures that have been developed on abuse, in response to the guidance, *No Secrets*, produced by the Department of Health (see Chapter 8).

It is important that the procedures are not overly bureaucratic and can easily be applied on a day-to-day basis. Procedures are sometimes seen as a necessary evil – but they are a tool to help all concerned and, in the case of financial matters, a vital element of protection and a safeguard for staff and service users. Home care managers should ensure that all their staff, including volunteers, as well as service users or their representatives, are given written information, from the outset, on the procedures that are in place on handling money or belongings. It may be necessary to remind people of these from time to time, especially if service users frequently ask the home care worker to undertake tasks that are outside, or contrary to, the procedures, or if they offer gifts of a more expensive nature than the procedures allow (see Chapter 7).

In looking at a whole range of situations, this book is intended to help those responsible for setting up their organisation's procedures on handling service users' money or belongings. It is important that all the possible scenarios are considered beforehand rather than waiting until a situation arises and being forced to react to it. However, it is inevitable that, no matter how detailed the procedures, new situations may arise which are not covered and that, from time to time, things will go wrong.

It must also be remembered that procedures by themselves do not protect service users, staff or volunteers. They point to good practice, and give staff and volunteers a clear idea of the ground rules within which they are working. Procedures are an important part of the whole ethos of the agency or department, in the way it goes about recruitment, training and supervision. Above all, managers should be aware that the way service users, staff and volunteers are valued will always count far more than any set of procedures on their own.

Writing the procedures

Those who write the procedures for home care workers' involvement with service users' financial affairs and belongings have to strike a delicate balance between trying to cover as many eventualities as possible, without being too long, bureaucratic or prescriptive. Standard 13 of the National Minimum Standards (see Appendix 1) lists the topics that must be covered by registered home care agencies.

Procedures should be clearly written and presented in a way that makes them easy to use and understand. This includes:

- giving reasons for the procedures;
- clear lay-out;
- simple, jargon-free language;
- easy ways of referencing (section, index or colour coding);
- easy ways of updating;
- clearly dating procedures once approved (and if/when updated).

It may be possible to get hold of a number of different examples of procedures from both local authorities and home care agencies for comparison. The staff who oversaw them could advise if any practical problems have been encountered, along with reasons why some material has intentionally been included or excluded.

Organisations that have a range of responsibilities to service users and their finances could consider a 'core' set of procedures, with a 'mix and match' approach to specific workers or situations. For example, home care workers from social services departments and sheltered housing staff who work in housing departments could be undertaking similar tasks in relation to service users' finances, yet both be working to different procedures. If this 'core' set of procedures were clearly divided into sections so that all staff were aware which were relevant to them, it would avoid duplication and keep required reading down to a minimum. Such a method would be helpful in presenting the overall picture to all home care workers and clarifying their roles and responsibilities.

Revising the procedures

The National Minimum Standards stipulate that policies and procedures are reviewed and amended annually, or more frequently if necessary. Opportunities to respond quickly to unexpected changes should be taken, otherwise staff may be unsure of how to proceed. For example, lottery scratch cards and supermarket reward cards are relatively new and so procedures for handling these may not have been included in the original documentation. The changes to payment arrangements planned by the Department for Work and Pensions (DWP – formerly the Department of Social Security), starting from 2003, could mean that procedures for collecting pensions and benefits will have to be altered once the new system comes into operation (see page 37).

Any revisions to procedures should be clearly dated. If the revisions replace the previous procedures (in whole or in part), home care workers should destroy those that are out of date. Managers should always keep one set of previous procedures for their records: this will be important if there is a complaint which covers a period of time, as highlighted in the Ombudsman case, 99/B/1651, in Appendix 2.

Consultation

When writing or revising procedures, a consultation process should be built in, and include both home care workers and service users. This will help ensure they are based on practical experience and give the procedures wider ownership. A home care agency that is starting up must have some procedures in place from the beginning, but should have the possibility for monitoring and evaluating them once they have been in operation for a few months.

As well as home care workers and service users, it is important to consult widely with representatives from other interested parties such as health providers, local social security offices (formerly the Benefits Agency), insurance companies, local solicitors, banks and trading standards departments of local authorities.

Care must be taken to ensure that the procedures comply with the law and the National Minimum Standards, and that they fall within the terms of any insurance policy in relation to home care workers handling service users' finances. The position of volunteers should be carefully considered, and included in any procedures.

Members of British Association of Domiciliary Care Officers (BADCO) or United Kingdom Home Care Association (UKHCA) will want to refer to their good practice guides and any code of practice. Charities will need to ensure that their procedures are within the terms of their charitable status and charity law. All care agencies will need to ensure that they comply with the codes of practice produced by the General Social Care Council (see page 4).

Agency contracts with local authorities

Private and voluntary home care agencies should have their own procedures. If an agency has a contract with the local authority, however, the agency's procedures will have to be agreed with the local authority before a contract is signed. Alternatively, it might be decided that the agency's staff will follow the local authority's own procedures. Agencies that contract with a number of local authorities may be faced with a range of differing procedures. The same principles apply, however, and there should be written agreement in each contract about which set of procedures are to be adopted to avoid any misunderstanding at a later date. All registered agencies providing personal care (see page 5) should have procedures that conform to the National Minimum Standards which come into effect from April 2003.

There could be times when an agency home care worker visits a service user both under contract to social services (the agency has been contracted to do certain work for the local authority) and because the service user has bought extra services from the agency outside of the social services' contract. Home care agencies and local authorities should have strategies in place to deal with this situation so that neither the home care worker nor the service user is unsure of their position. For example, there could be confusion about the acceptance of gifts at Christmas if one set of procedures allows small gifts and the other does not.

Who needs to know about the procedures?

All those who visit people in an official capacity on behalf of an organisation, including volunteers, need to be aware of any written procedures in relation to service users' money and belongings, and the requirement to follow them. The organisation's policy should be made clear to everyone on appointment. There should be signed confirmation that the procedures have been read by all those who will be visiting in an official capacity. Knowledge of procedures should be reinforced and updated regularly through training and supervision.

There should be full discussion and consultation if the procedures are revised. All concerned should sign the new procedures and destroy those that are now out of date. It is important that mechanisms are in place to ensure that all relevant personnel are made aware of revisions and updates as they occur.

The procedures may have to cover a wide range of situations for individual staff or volunteers who have varying levels of responsibility for service users' finances. These include:

- volunteers who are not expected to get involved directly with finances but who might become aware that the service user is getting into difficulties with their money because of growing confusion;
- home care workers who regularly shop and collect pensions and benefits for the service user;
- sheltered housing staff who have no involvement with their tenants' money but who collect and safeguard money for events within the scheme, such as outings;
- support workers in a group home who have responsibility for service users' pensions and benefits and are involved in helping them with their day-to-day budgeting.

Procedures should also be given to staff and volunteers, even if they would not normally be expected to have responsibility for service users' finances, as they may still have some involvement in the financial aspects of the service user's life. Examples include:

- a service user might ask a volunteer visitor for a loan to tide them over;
- a sheltered housing scheme manager, who does not normally deal with finances, may find the tenant unconscious, and have to take responsibility for locking the property and protecting that person's valuables if they are taken to hospital;
- a home care worker, not employed for shopping, may suddenly have to assume this role if they find that the service user is without food over a weekend due to a breakdown in arrangements.

What needs to be included?

The problem facing most writers of procedures is what to include. For registered home care agencies, certain items relating to handling money have to be in the procedures uner the National Minimum

Standards (see Appendix 1). In all cases, the principles behind the procedures should be clearly stated at the beginning.

It may be tempting to decide that some aspects of handling a service user's money are so obvious, they are not worth including. However, the consultation process should highlight that what may be obvious to one person may not be so to another. There is a danger that, if a point is not included in the procedures, staff may assume that it is permissible to undertake a particular action.

Case study

Hugh Davies, a sheltered housing schemes' manager, had written the procedures for staff handling tenants' finances. They were not encouraged to be involved unless absolutely necessary and the procedures were quite short – just dealing with shopping and collecting pensions and benefits in emergency situations. He later found that one of the sheltered housing workers, who had been shopping for a tenant, had been given the lady's PIN number and cash card so that she could get money from the cashpoint at the supermarket. Hugh had thought that no one would disclose their PIN number, given all the warnings given by banks and building societies to keep them confidential, so he had not put it into the guidance. When the tenant had offered the PIN number and cash card, the worker had assumed it was permissible for her to get money in that way, as there was nothing in the procedures. She just wanted to be helpful but had not thought about the implications of such an act, both for herself and the service user, had someone else also been given access and had misappropriated funds.

Consultation and discussion with line managers should always take place if home care workers are asked to do anything by the service user that is not in the procedures. It should make clear the differing levels of responsibility and accountability within the organisation in relation to handling money and dealing with the range of possible situations.

Although the procedures will need to cover a number of financial issues, not all will need a lengthy explanation and, in some cases, a short paragraph or even a sentence will suffice.

How prescriptive?

There are likely to be some points made in the procedures which must be strictly adhered to by the home care worker whatever the circumstances. There is a danger, however, that if procedures are too prescriptive, so that home care workers and service users consider that they hamper their day-to-day work, they might collude with each other to circumvent them. Home care workers should feel able to discuss special circumstances with their manager and the service user, who may allow some flexibility, provided any arrangements are agreed in writing.

Case study

Gerry, a home care worker, visits Mr Muldoon every morning to help him get up, and again in the evening to enable him to get back into bed. He also collects his pension on a weekly basis. Mr Muldoon is the first person Gerry visits in the morning and the last one at night. Gerry passes the post office (where Mr Muldoon's pension is paid) on the way to see him. He lives in a built-up area. It only takes Gerry five minutes to get from the post office to Mr Muldoon's house, but heavy traffic can mean a journey of as much as 20 minutes, if he has to pick up Mr Muldoon's pension book first. Mr Muldoon and Gerry both think this is a waste of time. It means that Gerry has very little time on the day he collects the pension to help Mr Muldoon get dressed. He does not have time to shave him. The procedures are clear that a home care worker should, under no circumstances, take pension books home with them. Gerry and Mr Muldoon decide that it makes more sense for Gerry to call into the post office to pick up the pension on his way in and so Mr Muldoon gives him the pension book on Wednesday nights. This is only discovered when Gerry is off sick one Thursday.

Because the procedures used the term 'under no circumstances', Gerry did not think it would be possible to discuss the situation with his manager to allow a variation. His manager, who is fully aware of the traffic problem, may have taken a pragmatic approach and agreed to this arrangement if all three (manager, home care worker and service user) signed that they were willing for this to happen and that the manager was satisfied that Gerry took appropriate care of the pension book whilst it was in his keeping.

Procedures should state which member of staff can authorise decisions that vary from those laid down. This could be staff of different levels of seniority, depending on the nature of any risks associated with a variation. They should also state whether the agreement of all concerned, including the service user, should be in writing and recorded in both the visit record, kept in the service user's home, and the office file.

Information for service users

It is important for the service user, or any person who has authority to deal with the service user's finances (see Chapter 5), to be aware that there are procedures, and that they should be given information in writing for reference. The National Minimum Standards make it a requirement for registered home care agencies that service users have access to relevant information on the policies and procedures and other documents, in appropriate formats.

Service users should be given an information leaflet that explains, in clear, jargon-free language, what the home care worker normally can and cannot do on their behalf, in relation to handling money and belongings. This should include details about the policy on confidentiality and the circumstances when it might need to be breached. The leaflet should explain the reasons for particular decisions, and reinforce any discussion that the manager has with the service user when the service first starts. It should help the service user to appreciate that these procedures are protecting their own interests, as well as those of the home care worker. Any changes to the procedures should include consultation with service users or their representatives, and be notified to all concerned.

Monitoring that procedures are followed

Procedures will only prove to be effective if they are regularly monitored to ensure they are being followed. The procedures should state how they will be monitored (such as regular checks on receipt books) and actions that will be taken in the event of them not being followed. Monitoring should not be allowed to lapse because of pressure of other work.

Service users should be made aware that the procedures are monitored and that their comments and views about the way they are followed will be valued. Service users should have details in writing about how they can make a complaint if they are not happy with the way their money is being handled or if procedures are not being followed. As some service users may find it difficult to complain about their home care worker, face-to-face interviews between the home care manager and the service user should also take place on a regular basis.

Case study

Marjorie Phillips had received several inaccurate receipts from her home care worker in the last few months. She had noticed items from shopping trips that she had not asked for and not received. Marjorie liked her home care worker and knew that she was under a lot of family pressure as her husband was very ill, so she had not wanted to take it up with her when signing for the goods. She knew she could complain but felt that a written complaint was too 'formal'. The home care manager, who had not been aware of this problem because the receipts all tallied in the receipt book, visited Marjorie as part of the regular quality assurance visits. This approach, which was routine, enabled Marjorie to express her concerns when she was invited to make comments on all aspects of the service, and enabled the manager to take appropriate action.

Ways of monitoring will vary, and may include:

- regular monitoring of paperwork;
- random visits to service users;
- investigation of any complaints.

Monitoring the handling of the service user's financial affairs is, of course, only one aspect of the management of staff and quality assurance of the service offered. Monitoring of procedure compliance should be regarded as a part of general staff management. It needs to fit in with the overall development of staff competence, through regular team meetings and one-to-one supervision, ensuring opportunities for discussion, feedback and training.

KEY POINTS FROM THIS CHAPTER

Do:

- have written procedures on handling finances;
- ensure that all those who visit service users, regardless of whether they are usually involved in financial matters, are aware of the procedures;
- ensure these procedures have been discussed, and signed as read;
- consult widely (including service users);
- know which set of procedures are to be followed, if working for an agency under contract to a local authority;
- ensure procedures are written in clear, accessible language, and dated;
- ensure regular discussion, supervision and training;
- revise procedures regularly to deal with new provisions;
- ensure that monitoring and evaluation are carried out regularly;
- ensure that service users have information about the procedures in an easily accessible form;
- ensure that service users know how to complain.

Don't:

- regard procedures as a negative – they should be there to protect and help;
- ignore or deviate from the procedures, even if service users want this, without full discussion and the manager's agreement;
- only alter the procedures in response to a complaint – there should be regular reviews;
- rely totally on the procedures on their own to protect service users and home care workers – use discussion and training, and monitoring.

2 Financial transactions

This chapter covers money or goods transactions between the service user and the home care worker. These include shopping and the collection of pensions and benefits. In the case of sheltered housing workers, it could include collecting money for social events or TV licences. There may also be occasions when home care workers pay bills on behalf of the service user or are involved with the banking of money. Each of these is covered in a separate section later in the chapter. It starts, however, by considering general principles relating to home care workers handling money or goods to ensure that the service user is as much in control as possible and that the possibility for misunderstandings is kept to an absolute minimum.

Initial considerations

Home care workers should only be involved in financial transactions if no other practical options are available which are acceptable to the service user, and all other means of providing the assistance have been explored. When the home care service is provided by a local authority or home care agency, the nature and extent of the financial transactions will normally be drawn up as part of the care plan.

- Home care agencies providing personal care must have policies and procedures, in compliance with Standard 13 of the National Minimum Standards (see Appendix 1).
- All home care workers should be aware, and have up-to-date copies, of procedures that have been drawn up concerning financial transactions.

- These procedures should be read and discussed as part of the home care worker's induction and signed by them and their manager after discussion.
- Regular discussion of what is required by the procedures should be built into supervision or team meetings.

Whilst procedures normally cover those situations when there are regular financial transactions, there will be times when they are necessary on a one off-basis, perhaps because the family carer is away or the service user is ill. Procedures need to be in place that give guidance to home care workers on what they should do in these circumstances, particularly if there has been no prior warning that a financial transaction will be necessary.

Case study

Maureen Carter, a home care worker, finds Mrs Walen very worried. Her daughter usually collects her pension and does her shopping for her on Thursdays but has rung to say she has a very bad viral infection, and has been told by her doctor that she must stay in bed. Mrs Walen does not have any money left and is running short of some food. Her neighbours, who might have been able to help, are on holiday until next Tuesday and her granddaughter cannot pop in until the weekend, as she lives too far away. Although it is not in the care plan to collect pensions or do shopping, Maureen knows that her agency's procedures will allow her to do so, if necessary. Whilst Mrs Walen writes out a shopping list and signs the pension book, Maureen rings through to the agency to explain the situation. Her manager gives authorisation, which is recorded on the case file. The agency issues all home care workers with a spare receipt book to cover such temporary situations, so Maureen is able to issue a receipt for the transactions in the same way as she does for those for whom she regularly shops.

If home care workers are employed directly by the service user, it is important to agree in writing what financial transactions will be undertaken by the home care worker, if no other suitable options exist.

Handling money or goods

It is vital that the service user agrees that the transaction is accurate and complies with their wishes. (See Chapter 5 for what to do if service users are mentally incapable of managing their own affairs.) Although some service users may be quite happy to suggest that the home care worker takes money for shopping from their purse, this could cause problems later if there is a dispute about how much has been taken. Equally, if goods that have been purchased are simply put away by the home care worker, the service user may not be sure if all the items requested have been bought.

To avoid this, any money and/or goods that change hands between the service user and home care worker should be checked by the service user. Only money that has been counted out by the service user (or the home care worker in front of the service user) should be accepted and receipted. Goods bought should be checked by the service user against the receipts from the shops before being put away. Service users should then sign for the receipt of those goods.

Dealing with coins and notes

Money handed over to the service user should be carefully counted either into the service user's hand or onto a table or other suitable area where the service user can see it and check it. Particular care needs to be taken to ensure that service users with sight or hearing problems are satisfied that the transaction is correct. The Royal National Institute of the Blind (see Appendix 4) can give advice and assistance to aid coin and note recognition. Where possible, service users with a visual impairment should be encouraged to write down the amount themselves when signing for money, so they are sure that they are signing for the amount they have received. If this is not possible, it should be suggested to the service user that, if they wish, they show the receipts to a person they trust to ensure that the amount tallies with what they believe they are signing for. Managers should also check receipts, taking particular care when checking those of people who have sight problems.

Some service users find it difficult to manage certain coins (the five pence coin, for example, as it is so small) because of problems with fine finger movement. Efforts should be made to establish service user's preferences and, as far as possible, change should be in denominations that the service user finds easiest to manage.

When new coins or bank notes are about to be introduced, it is useful to alert service users to the fact that they might come across money that they do not recognise. Once they have a new coin or note, the home care worker should make a point of showing it to the service user and stating its value.

Particular care should be given if the service user's first language is not English. They may find it difficult to understand if money is counted out quickly in English, and it may be more helpful for the service user to count out the money themselves. Learning a few key phrases and numbers in the service user's language could help considerably, if the home care worker is not from the same ethnic background.

Keeping receipts

All receipts should be returned to the service user and systems should be set up (in the form of a cash/receipt or account book) for both the service user and home care worker to record and sign the transaction. There should be a copy available for the service user to keep, as well as the home care provider. The National Minimum Standards state that these should remain in the service user's home for a minimum of one month (or until the service is concluded), after which they can be transferred, with the service user's agreement, for safe keeping.

The use of the receipt book, and what to do if a mistake is made or the book lost, should be covered by procedures. Decisions need to be made about the length of time a completed receipt book should be kept and where it should be stored to comply with the Data Protection Act 1998 and other statutory requirements. The National Minimum Standards state that the requisite length of time for keeping accounts and details of financial transactions is seven years.

Using a service user's goods

There should be clear procedures in place concerning the use of a service user's belongings. For example, service users should not be expected to bear the cost of any telephone calls made by a home care worker. Use of the service user's phone should always be discouraged. If it *is* used (in an emergency, for example), there should be clear accounting procedures to reimburse service users when the call is not in relation to the service user's needs.

If a home care package involves staff being in the service user's home at mealtimes and there is an expectation that the home care worker will need to eat there, clear accounting arrangements should be in place to pay for the food consumed by staff. Service users should not be expected to bear the cost.

Home care workers should never borrow money or goods from service users – and equally never lend money or goods.

Safekeeping service user's property

Once service users hand money, cheques or pension and benefits books to their home care worker, they have put that worker in a position of trust. It is vital that the home care worker takes care, both to keep the service user's money or goods safe and to protect themselves.

Ideally, a home care worker should only deal with one service user's transactions at a time. In any event, it is important for the home care worker to keep their own money separate from that of the service user at all times. If work routines mean staff undertake financial transactions for several service users together, each service user's money should be accounted for separately. The money held for each service user and the receipts obtained should be clearly identifiable for each individual. Consideration must be given, in these circumstances, to the safekeeping of any items bought whilst delivering goods to the other service users (see Chapter 6).

Any money or goods collected for the service user should be given to them as soon as possible on the same day. If for any reason this is not possible, arrangements should be in place for authorising the holding of goods or money, and for suitable safe storage.

Home care workers should not be put in a position of having to carry large amounts of cash. Upper limits should be in place, stating the maximum amount of service user's cash they should be expected to carry. This should be in line with insurance cover. Special procedures may be needed when pensions and benefits are collected over a bank holiday or Christmas, for example, when two weeks are paid, which could easily take the amounts over any maximum limit.

Case study

A manager of a sheltered housing scheme had agreed to collect the money for an outing on which tenants in her scheme were going. The day out included a meal and the entry fee to a stately home, which came to £20 per tenant. It took time to collect the money from the 50 tenants in the scheme. The manager kept the money in a cash-box in her flat until it could be banked. When her supervisor found out, she was very concerned that the manager had been responsible for £1,000, which was above the household contents insurance cover for cash, and that she had made no special arrangements when going to the bank. The manager herself had been worried and had slept with it under her pillow until she could get to the bank the following day. It made the supervisor realise that, although the policy was that sheltered housing managers did not deal with tenants' financial arrangements such as shopping and collecting benefits, this part of the task had not been properly addressed.

Confidentiality

It is a requirement of the National Minimum Standards (see Appendix 1) that registered home care agencies have written policies and procedures on confidentiality, specifying the circumstances under which confidentiality may be breached, and the process for dealing with inappropriate breaches. Wherever possible, all financial transactions undertaken for service users should remain confidential, and information handled in accordance with the Data Protection Act 1998 and the agency's policies and procedures. Home care workers should be aware of the circumstances when information given to them in confidence must be shared with their manager and other social/health care agencies. Service users should also be made aware of these and have summaries of the agency's policies and procedures on confidentiality. If the home care worker is told something in confidence that they consider they must disclose, the service user should always be told, and given the reasons for disclosure and to whom the information will be given.

As service users are in their own homes, in the majority of cases there will be no problems in ensuring privacy in the handing over of cash and goods. Home care workers need to be careful if someone else, such as a friend, relative or other professional, is visiting when they plan to hand over money or goods to the service user. The service user should be in control, and cash or goods should not be handed over in the presence of another person unless the service user has given the home care worker express permission to do so.

Shopping

Wherever possible, the service user should be supported to do their own shopping rather than having it done for them, and this should form part of the care plan. Often, though, time constraints mean that it is quicker for day-to-day shopping to be done by the home care worker. It must be remembered, however, that, for some people, shopping is a social activity rather than a chore to be avoided. Even supermarket shopping may bring about a meeting between old friends, or a chat with a friendly checkout assistant, which can help lessen social isolation.

Other possibilities should be explored before the home care worker takes on this task. These should include the use of 'Dial-a-Ride' (a transport service for people with disabilities), shopmobility schemes (which provide a buggy or scooter and often have volunteers to assist the person), or whether there are relatives or friends who could accompany and help the service user with their shopping. Enabling people to shop for themselves, with assistance, may enhance their independence. Transport and vehicle insurance must be considered if home care workers take service users shopping in their own car.

'Tele-shopping' is a relatively new way of purchasing goods and services, and home delivery is an increasingly common service offered by retailers. These may be worth exploring with the service user, but should not be used purely for the convenience of the agency or local authority staff, especially if the service user would like to have the opportunity to shop, is able (or can be enabled) to do so and would benefit from the social activity.

If a service user has difficulty shopping, it may be possible for the home care worker to do the day-to-day shopping and just occasionally take the service user with them, or encourage a relative or friend to do so. This should be written into the care plan, following an assessment of the risks involved in the person being supported to go shopping.

For some people, however, the only option may be for home care workers to shop on their behalf. There is the danger that, without seeing new items and products, the service user will find it difficult to think of variations to what can become a limited shopping list and diet. The home care worker can play a crucial role in giving people who are housebound ideas of items they have seen, which they think the older person may like to try, and keeping them in touch with new products or the seasonal variations in food items that are in the shops.

Choice

If someone is unable to do their shopping, it is vital that they should be allowed to keep their preferences over where their shopping is done and the items that are bought. Some people prefer to use local shops, even though they may be more expensive than supermarkets or have a smaller range of goods. Home care workers should point out if there are differences in prices that they think the service user may not be aware of, but the choice should always be the service user's.

Case study

Mrs Brooks is housebound and has her shopping done by Carole, her home care worker, once a week at a supermarket. Mrs Brooks likes certain brands, and prefers to buy small quantities, even though she knows they are more expensive. Carole is aware of this and meticulously follows instructions. Another home care worker does Mrs Brooks' shopping one week. She takes the list Mrs Brooks has made out, but returns with the supermarket's own brands, and a large packet of cornflakes, as it was on special offer. She made a point of telling Mrs Brooks what bargains she had got. Mrs Brooks did not see it in the same light – it would take her weeks to get through such a large packet of cornflakes. In the end, she had to throw half the packet away.

Home care workers should also be sensitive to service user's religious beliefs, and be rigorous about shopping in appropriate shops, only buying items which fit in with those beliefs (unless requested to do otherwise by the service user). They should also take care that the handling, storage, preparation and cooking of food conform to any beliefs. These principles should also apply to a service user's political beliefs – for example, not buying from companies that have policies that the service user does not like.

There may be times when it is impossible for the home care worker to use the shop of choice – perhaps because of the distance between each shop, or unusual or varying opening hours. This will need to be resolved by negotiation between the service user and home care manager. Decisions need to be made, and agreed by all concerned, about shopping at places where it is difficult to obtain receipts, such as market stalls, if this is the service user's preference.

Choice and risk

Service users are free to ask for items that they wish to spend their money on. These may not always seem sensible or desirable to the home care worker, but it is up to the individual how they spend their money. Home care workers can suggest items to help a balanced diet, or offer more choice, but should accept what the service user puts on their list.

Procedures should be in place for the home care worker if they have particular concerns about the purchases made by the service user. There may be occasions, for example, when particular purchases may be thought to be of risk to the service user, such as alcohol for a person with a known alcohol problem; ordinary sweets for someone with diabetes; or over-the-counter tablets such as paracetamol for someone who has previously made suicide attempts. There is a delicate balance between the individual's right to choose, and the duty of care to ensure that nothing is done by the home care worker that will harm that individual.

The National Minimum Standards (see Appendix 1) stipulate that limitations on the chosen lifestyle or human rights to prevent self-harm or self-neglect, or abuse or harm to others, are made only in the service user's best interest, consistent with the agency's responsibilities in law. The limitations should only follow a risk assessment and the plan for managing the risks, and entered into the service user's plan.

Ideally, potential problems about particular items will have been identified, and agreement about how this will be handled, from the outset. There may be times when it is necessary to tell the service user that it is not considered to be in their interest to use the home care worker to buy certain items. Refusal to buy items of the service user's choice should only occur following discussion with the service user, the care manager and the home care worker's manager and, if it is considered that their health is being put at risk, the service user's general practitioner (GP).

Advice should be sought from any specialist teams and, if possible, the service user offered support from them. Care must be taken that such decisions are not made on the basis of the standards and beliefs of the home care worker, but on an assessment of the real risk posed to the service user by their behaviour. All decisions in cases such as these should be carefully recorded and discussed with the service user.

Establishing the items a service user wants

Any shopping list should be written by or with the service user, and include information about brands and quantity. Where appropriate, it should include substitute items in case the service user's choice is not available.

The home care worker should be particularly aware of dietary or cultural requirements when helping the service user plan their shopping list. If a service user has a restricted diet, suggestions could be made to vary this, where appropriate. Reminders may be necessary if the service user is becoming a bit forgetful about family birthdays or other special occasions that they may wish to celebrate or be involved with in some way. It may be helpful to make a note of all the important dates on a wall calendar, which home care workers can check.

If shopping is done on a regular basis and the service user has difficulty in writing, the home care worker could help compile a list of what they are likely to need on a regular basis. This could be photocopied so the service user just ticks which of the regular items is needed, and only has to add a few items that are required less frequently.

Checking the goods purchased

As well as ensuring that service users have agreed that the change is correct, it is important that they are given the opportunity to check the goods bought. This is particularly so if they are not able to put away the goods themselves or have sight problems. Home care workers need to ensure that the service user has had a chance to check the items, knows exactly where they have been put and has been told of any 'use by' dates for perishable goods.

If other people come in to cook for the service user, it may be necessary to work out ways of ensuring that everybody is aware of the items that have been bought and what should be used quickly and not left at the back of the fridge. It may be helpful to leave a list of what has been put in the fridge and how soon it should be used. This is particularly important if the service user is forgetful.

Financial aspects of shopping

The home care worker should not make any gain – or loss – from undertaking shopping for service users. For example, procedures need to cover the use of time, such as the home care worker doing their own shopping whilst shopping for service users.

Home care workers should not use their own money or credit cards to buy goods for the service user. If the service user clearly does not have enough money, on occasions, to buy all the essential items, procedures need to be in place to ensure that they can be purchased without the home care worker sustaining any loss.

Service users should be encouraged to give slightly more money than seems necessary to cover price rises and a possible miscalculation of the amount needed. If it is not too costly or time-consuming, a home care agency may wish to consider setting up a small float for home care workers who shop regularly. This could ensure that essential items can be purchased, even if the service user has not handed over (or does not have) enough money. The service user would be expected to replace any money spent from the float.

REWARD CARDS AND SPECIAL OFFERS

Many shops and supermarkets have brought in reward card schemes, air miles and other incentives that the service user might wish to make use of. Procedures should be in place to cover the use of such incentive schemes that belong to the service user as the purchaser of the goods. These would include home care workers finding out if the service user is a member (or would like to be one), and taking any relevant cards with them when shopping at the store concerned. There are also reductions and special offers such as 2 for 1, which the service user should be made aware of, wherever possible, so they can make a decision whether they wish to make use of these. Home care workers must not use their own reward cards when purchasing goods for service users, even if the service user does not already have or want a reward card.

LOTTERY TICKETS AND SCRATCH CARDS

There are also issues to be considered concerning lottery tickets and scratch cards, which home care workers are now sometimes asked to buy. It is particularly important to be aware of potential problems, if home care workers buy lottery scratch cards for themselves or other people at the same time as for the service user – if there is a winning card, the service user could query whose card it was. If procedures are already in place that the home care worker should not shop for themselves whilst shopping for service users, they may need to make it clear that this includes lottery scratch cards.

With regard to the national lottery, it is advisable for service users to choose their own numbers in advance and for tickets to be handed over to the service user and not left for the home care worker to check. Procedures may also need to consider home care workers being asked to randomly check tickets and/or collect any winnings. There should also be procedures about lottery syndicates, which are referred to in Standard 13 of the National Minimum Standards (see Appendix 1).

TAKING ITEMS FOR REPAIR

On occasion, the service user may ask the home care worker to take items for repair. Normal receipting arrangements should be in place to show that the item has been taken to the repairers. Procedures also need to cover situations when the item is of greater value than is covered by the agency's insurance cover (see Chapter 6).

SELLING GOODS OR SERVICES

Standard 13 of the National Minimum Standards (see Appendix 1) makes it clear that home care workers should not sell goods or services to, or on behalf of, the service user, and that procedures should be in place to cover this. Such procedures should include selling through mail order, when the home care worker may receive commission.

Payment of pensions and benefits

Before home care workers undertake any regular collection of pensions and benefits, there should be discussion with the service user to see if there is anyone else who could undertake this or if any other method of payment could be used.

Pensions and benefits that are cashed at the post office are paid either by an order book (sometimes called pension book or benefit order book) or giro cheque (giro). It is important to ensure that benefit orders or giros are cashed within the time limits allowed by the regulations. This is three months for a benefit order and one month for a giro. After this time, replacements have to be issued, although the payment is cancelled after 12 months unless there are exceptional circumstances. Once the benefit order has been encashed, there is no liability by the Department for Work and Pensions (previously known as the Department of Social Security) if that money is lost or misappropriated.

It is planned to gradually end the use of order books, which are still a popular method of receiving pensions and benefits. All pensions and benefits will start to be paid into bank accounts. For people who do not have a bank account, pensions and benefits can still be obtained through a new card account run by the post office, or from one of the participating banks' basic bank accounts, also through the post office network.

The service user might wish to consider the possibility of having pensions and benefits paid directly into the bank, before the order books are phased out. This could enable the service user to keep more control and confidentiality of their financial affairs, if they do not need to have someone collecting their money each week. For those people who cannot get to a bank, consideration should be given to how they can access their money from the bank, such as through the use of suitable cashpoints. No one should be pressured into a payment method that they do not wish to use, however.

Case study

Mrs Welsh can no longer get to the post office to collect her pension and benefits. She likes having the weekly cash, and used to enjoy meeting her friends in the post office. She cannot see the point in having her pension and benefits paid into the bank, as she would still need someone to get the money out of the bank. She is not keen on anyone knowing how much she gets. Her son works and would find it difficult to get to the bank when it is open. However, her son takes her shopping once a week in the evening or at the weekend. Mrs Welsh had never really taken much notice of the cashpoints at the supermarket. When she realises that, if she had the money paid into the bank, she could draw out the money either at the cashpoint or using a debit card at the checkout, she decides that it could be quite a good idea.

Collecting pensions and benefits

If a service user still needs someone to collect their pensions and benefits on their behalf, they can appoint an agent (see below). To do so, they must be able to understand the nature of the agreement – if they are becoming too confused to manage their own affairs, other arrangements will be needed (see Chapter 5). Home care workers are most likely to act in the capacity of an agent, unless they work in a particular scheme supporting people in the community who lack capacity.

If the home care worker regularly collects the service user's pensions and benefits, this should be indicated on the care plan. Procedures should be in place to cover such arrangements, as well as times when a home care worker undertakes it on an occasional basis, and it is not part of the care plan. Arrangements should include whether home care workers become casual or standing agents (these are outlined below). However, it should be noted that the current way that agents collect pensions and benefits is likely to change when the new system of paying pensions and benefits into a bank account is phased in between 2003 and 2005, and new procedures will be necessary.

CASUAL AGENTS

Casual agents can be nominated on a temporary basis to cover occasions when the service user is not personally able to get to the post office. The service user has to complete the declaration and authorisation in their order book each time. The casual agent also has to sign and date a statement on the back of the payment slip confirming that the person is alive, that they have received the amount printed on the order and that they will pay that amount to the person whose name is on the front of the order straight away. It is likely that there will different procedures as the payment arrangements change from 2003 onwards.

STANDING AGENTS

A standing agent is often used when pensions and benefits need to be collected each week on a regular basis. The service user can nominate a person as a standing agent and ask the social security office to issue that agent with an agency card (BF74). The card shows that that person is authorised to collect money for the claimant, and the card is used as identification each time a benefit is collected. The service user still has to sign each order due for payment. As it is the individual home care worker who becomes the standing agent, it is only appropriate when they visit the service user regularly. Staff turnover may mean that it is inappropriate to nominate home care workers as standing agents. If a standing agent is away temporarily, the service user can ask another home care worker to be a casual agent for that time.

ℹ For further information on agency arrangements, see the Department for Work and Pensions' information leaflet, A *helping hand with benefits: a guide for agents and appointees.*

ℹ See also Age Concern Factsheet 22 *Legal arrangements for managing financial affairs.*

Responsibilities of an agent

Home care workers should be aware of the limits of their responsibilities as an agent, even if they only occasionally collect pensions and benefits for service users. The responsibilities are the same for both casual and standing agents and merely authorise the agent to collect pensions and benefits on the service user's behalf.

Home care workers acting as agents should ensure that a service user is aware of the exact amount collected each week. Normally the amounts are the same each week but there are times, particularly when the pensions and benefits are uprated in April of each year, that they alter. The money should be handed over to the service user or only spent if the service user has given permission to do so, such as to buy shopping out of the amount collected. Receipting arrangements for pensions and benefits must be in place.

Home care workers should always be issued with identification cards by their employer, and should always present them to the post office when collecting pensions and benefits. Self-employed home care workers will need some other form of identification. This may also be required in addition to the standing agent's card (BF74).

If a home care worker has been acting as an agent for some time, this arrangement should be regularly monitored. The care plan should include regular reviews, which should cover whether the service user is still capable of managing their financial affairs. It may be necessary to end the agency arrangement and to put a more appropriate arrangement into place (see Chapter 5).

Responsibilities of a service user

A service user must be able to choose who they want to be their agent, and they should only nominate someone they know they can trust, as there is currently no provision to regulate or monitor the use of agents.

The service user remains responsible for all matters relating to their pension and benefits. For example, it is service users not agents who are responsible for notifying the appropriate social security office of any change of circumstance that might affect pensions and benefits. However, home care workers can usefully point out to the service user the need to inform social security about any change of circumstance. Service users also remain responsible for making a claim for any other benefit to which they might be entitled (see Chapter 4 for a summary of the benefits commonly claimed by service users).

If the standing agency arrangement ends, for whatever reason, the service user must notify the social security office and return the agency card to the appropriate office immediately. The home care worker or service provider should check that this has happened and ensure it is recorded on the service user's file. Where appropriate, the service user may need to apply for another named home care worker to be their standing agent.

Safety issues

If home care workers collect pensions and benefits and carry cash regularly on behalf of the service user, they should consider what safety precautions they should take to protect both themselves and the service user. These could include not wearing a uniform when collecting pensions and benefits, and varying the time of collection. Home care workers should also take care not to make unguarded remarks when they are waiting at the post office, for example, as these could be overheard by someone who may know the service user or be interested in finding out if there is money in a particular person's home.

Case study

Angela regularly collects benefits for Mrs Dubrovski. One day, whilst in the queue, she met with another home care worker who she used to work with in social services but who now works for a private provider. They had a chat about the difference between working for social services and the independent sector. They did not appreciate that another person in the queue was listening to their conversation and realised that they were home care workers. Angela was followed back to Mrs Dubrovski's house, which was burgled that night, and a large amount of cash taken.

If the home care worker is concerned that the money collected is mounting up in the service user's home, this should be raised with the service user, pointing out the dangers of having a lot of money in the house and making suggestions for safe keeping. If this continues, it may be advisable to alert the home care manager.

Home care workers should return the pension and benefits order books immediately, as they are the property and responsibility of the service user. Any exceptions to this should only be made with the written agreement of the service user, home care worker and manager. It is up to the service user to ensure that their pensions and benefits books are safe within their home. However, if the home care worker has any worries about where they are kept, this should be pointed out to the service user and suggestions made for a safer place.

Bills

This section looks at home care workers paying bills and dealing with banking arrangements on behalf of service users. As with all financial transactions, every effort should be made to ensure that the service user does not have to involve their home care worker in their private billing and banking transactions, if other ways can be found which are acceptable to them.

Each service user will usually have a range of household bills that need to be paid regularly: rent, Council Tax, TV licence, gas, electricity, water, home and contents insurance etc. In addition, there will be the one-off bills such as for items that have to be replaced or to pay for a holiday.

The range of payment methods for bills

Large organisations, in particular the public utilities such as water, gas and electricity companies, have a growing range of methods of payment. For example, some services now offer Payment Cards rather than stamps, as this is thought to be a safer payment method. Some have payment facilities through home/telephone banking services. Some offer discounts for prompt payment and direct debit, or facilities where no bank charges are made if paid into certain banks. Home care workers should be aware of the different payment arrangements that organisations offer, so that they can draw these to the attention of the service user. Some organisations will give talks to staff on a range of issues, including methods of paying bills.

Paying the bills

Procedures need to be in place that specifically cover receipting arrangements for paying bills. Wherever possible, the home care worker should pay the bills at a place where a receipt is given. Records should always be kept of the amount that has been paid, either by cash or cheque, and the receipt given to the service user. Home care workers should know whether it is permissible to leave the payment in the collection boxes at the various public utility or store showrooms. Whilst this method avoids the necessity to queue, it means that there is no receipt immediately available for the service user.

Sometimes home care workers will be asked to post payments on behalf of service users. Home care workers should remind the service user to request a receipt from the organisation or company concerned. Once items have been posted, the home care worker should make a note of this on the service user's visit record. Care should be taken that bills do not get mixed up with other post that the home care worker may have for the service user. Posting the payment for bills is just as important as paying bills over the counter, as the service user could lose out financially or risk having the service cut off if there is a delay.

Although standing orders and direct debits can be an easy way for service users to pay their regular bills, home care workers need to be alert to the fact that things can sometimes go wrong. It may be that a standing order was set up based on a particularly high or low level of consumption of fuel, causing growing credit or debt. The service user may need some help in approaching the specific utility and arranging for the payment to be based on the current level of consumption.

If the service user receives Income Support/Minimum Income Guarantee (MIG) (see Chapter 4) and is in arrears, the Department for Work and Pensions can, in some cases, make direct payments to various utilities from Income Support/MIG. Although it is fairly unusual now, this method of payment should be explored when there are arrears. An amount is taken to cover the arrears, as well as to pay for current consumption. It is important that service users are aware that they need to keep a check on when the arrears have been paid off, and inform the social security office, which may otherwise deduct more than is necessary.

Unpaid bills

Procedures should be in place for home care workers if they become aware of a problem with unpaid bills. It is important that the service user is helped to deal with these at an early stage and the appropriate level of advice obtained for them. In some cases, the unpaid bills may be the result of the early stages of mental incapacity or depression, or because there is financial abuse and the service user has been pressured into giving away money put aside for bills. In other cases there might be a particular financial problem that may require money advice. Home care workers should be clear when they need to refer the matter to their manager who, in turn, may need to refer for expert help after discussion with the service user.

Banking

The exact level of involvement of home care workers in the service user's banking arrangements (which includes building societies) needs careful consideration and clear procedures. When a service user has the capacity to manage their own affairs, any involvement should be kept to an absolute minimum (see Chapter 5 for situations when service users are not able to manage their own affairs). The care plan should always state clearly what banking tasks the home care worker will undertake.

Putting money into the service user's account

The normal receipting arrangements should be followed so that the amount of money (either cash or cheques) taken from the service user's home has been agreed and signed, and a receipt (normally the cashier's stamp on the paying-in slip with the amount) is returned. Special procedures should be developed to ensure that service users who have sight problems can check the paying-in slips.

The amount of cash or cheques carried should be within the limits laid down by home care providers for staff to carry. Self-employed or directly-employed home care workers should check whether their insurance (or the service user's insurance) covers them to carry the service users' money and, if so, what the limit would be. Special arrangements may be needed if the service user has a large cheque or giro to be paid into the bank. When this is known in advance (for example, the service user has won an appeal for Attendance Allowance that has taken a long period to resolve, and backpayment is for several thousand pounds), the home care worker should explore with the service user ways it could be paid directly into an account. It may be useful for the home care worker to seek authority from their manager to help the service user open a bank account, if the service user has not yet got one, and to get advice on high interest accounts.

i The British Bankers Association provides information leaflets on opening bank accounts, banking products and services, and banking arrangements for people with a disability. See Appendix 4 for contact details.

Withdrawing money

Sometimes service users will need the help of home care workers to withdraw money from their accounts. This should always be done in a way that strictly limits the home care worker's access to the service user's bank account. It should normally be recorded on the care plan that the home care worker has been asked to withdraw money, the method by which this will be done, and the usual amounts that will be withdrawn. Each withdrawal should be separately recorded.

If a home care worker is asked to withdraw money from a service user's account because the normal arrangements have broken down, procedures should be in place for the home care worker to get permission from their organisation and for details of the transaction to be recorded on the service user's file, as well as through the normal receipting procedures.

Banks and building societies each have their own procedures for enabling a person, who is not the account holder, to withdraw money on the service user's behalf. The most common way is for the service user to sign a cheque for the amount they want cashed and give a letter of authorisation for the home care worker to present to the cashier. This letter can either be written each time, or a standing authority can be given, if the collection is regular, depending on the policy of the bank. This may not be appropriate if there are frequent changes of home care worker. The former has the advantage that the amount will be written in and the authorisation dated. A general authorisation may be considered too open, even if it places a limit on what can be withdrawn at any one time. The home care worker will, in addition, need to present some form of personal identification on each occasion. What is accepted will vary according to the rules of the bank or building society.

Security and banking

Any other form of withdrawal of money (such as a third party mandate allowing the home care worker to become a signatory on behalf of the service user, or the use of cash cards and PIN numbers) would give the home care worker far greater access to the person's account and leave both the service user and home care worker at risk if anything went wrong. Such practices should not be encouraged and procedures need to reflect this, especially in relation to normal banking practice and recommendations on cash card security.

Most banks and building societies make it quite clear in their leaflets that cards should not be given to anyone else and that PIN numbers should remain secret, even from bank staff or the police. Service users need to be aware that banks and building societies have strict rules about the cardholder's liability, if they have allowed somebody else access to their card or PIN number. Home care workers should refuse to accept PIN numbers, even if they are offered.

Home care workers need to be clear whether being a signatory, or using cash cards or PIN numbers, are subjects on which there is an absolute ban or if there are exceptional circumstances when it is open to the discretion of the manager, in agreement with the service user and home care worker, and no other solution can be found.

Case study

Jack English is completely housebound and wants to give Cynthia Hills, his home care worker, his PIN number with his cash card, as the local bank has recently closed. There is a cashpoint at a nearby supermarket. He is most insistent, as he feels that he should be allowed to take the risks if he wants to and he trusts Cynthia. Cynthia talks it over with her manager, but the procedures are quite clear that PIN numbers should never be given to home care workers. It is recognised as a problem, as Cynthia now spends a long time getting to the bank to get cash for Mr English so that she can do his shopping and get him some cash for the rest of the week. It reduces the time that she has to undertake other care tasks.

In spite of Mr English being happy to hand over his PIN number, after a case conference with his care manager, social services reluctantly agree to increase the number of hours of his care package so that Cynthia has time to go to the bank. All other options had been explored such as opening up a specific account with only a small amount of money in it. It was felt that, although Cynthia was a trusted worker, it would not be wise for Mr English to go against established banking advice and give out his PIN number.

If exceptions *are* ever made, the service user needs to agree to the arrangement in writing and be fully informed of the risks. Staff should have clear guidance. Managers need to keep very careful records if home care workers could have access to service users' accounts.

KEY POINTS FROM THIS CHAPTER

Do:

- only become involved with handling a service user's money after all other possibilities have been explored;
- keep rigorously to receipting and accounting procedures that are set up;
- make sure service users have counted out the money and know how much they are signing for;
- help service users retain choice over how their money is spent;
- involve the service user with what products are in the shops and inform them of new items as they appear;
- be sensitive to religious and political beliefs when shopping, or handling, storing and preparing food for the service user;
- keep each service user's money separate;
- maintain confidentiality at all times, in line with any written policies;
- be aware of the responsibilities of agents, and monitor that it is still appropriate for the service user to have an agent;
- make sure any bills to be mailed are posted promptly.

Don't:

- ignore the procedures that have been set up to protect staff and service users, even when there is a trusting relationship;
- discuss a service user's financial matters if there is anyone else in their home, unless the service user has given express permission to do so;
- expect service users to bear any costs that are not related to their needs (such as phone calls or food for staff);
- borrow from service users, or lend them money;
- rush the handing over of money or the checking of goods bought;
- use the service user's reward card points on goods for anyone else;
- carry more money or goods on behalf of the service user than laid down in procedures (or covered in home contents insurance for self-employed workers);
- take a service user's cash card and PIN number.

3 Self-employed or directly-employed home care workers

Many home care workers are employed either by local authorities or by independent home care agencies. These workers are supported by management structures and work to the policies and procedures of their organisations. Other home care workers, however, will be working alone, either self-employed or employed directly by the person needing care or support at home. Some will provide care to a number of different people during the course of a week, others might be employed to offer personal care as part of a 24-hour round-the-clock care package to one person. They are often called 'personal assistants' rather than home care workers. This chapter looks at points relating specifically to being self-employed or directly-employed, although all the chapters will be of relevance to those who are handling money.

Most of these home care workers will have a private arrangement, being paid by the individual to undertake agreed tasks. Both the individual needing care and the home care worker should come to their own agreement about how they work together. They are unlikely to have any support networks or procedures in place should problems occur.

Self-employed or directly-employed home care workers, who have been introduced to the service user by an employment agency, should be aware that these agencies have to comply with some of the National Minimum Standards. Those relating to financial issues outlined in this book have been reproduced in Appendix 1 and marked with an asterisk (*) if applicable to employment agencies.

Ground rules

Although home care workers who are self-employed or employed directly by older people are not normally bound by organisational procedures, it is important to consider setting some ground rules, in writing, if handling money will be an integral (or even occasional) part of the job. This could be in the contract of employment or conditions of service, if it is a formal arrangement, or a jointly agreed list between employer and employee. It is essential that the key principles in handling money or belongings, outlined in the introduction on page 9, should underpin the work of all home care workers.

Some older people will have considered the issues for themselves and be very clear in the way they wish all tasks, including financial tasks, to be undertaken. Others may not have given the matter any thought. In the latter case, the home care worker should raise the issues and invite discussion, especially if the service user seems uncertain about giving instructions, or appears not to realise that they are putting themselves or the home care worker at risk. A careful explanation of why the home care worker thinks it important to undertake financial tasks in a particular way, such as getting and recording receipts and not having PIN numbers, should help the home care worker and employer come to an agreement that safeguards them both.

If the home care worker has previously worked for a home care service provider, they should be familiar with the range of issues they need to cover. Others may not have had that experience, or have had a long break away from such organisations. The National Minimum Standards (see Appendix 1) may be a useful starting point in thinking about financial issues. It could also be useful for these workers to ask local home care providers for copies of their procedures so that they can think about the issues they need to cover when discussing how to handle financial matters with the person who has employed them. Many social services departments and other providers also produce leaflets highlighting issues for users of their services, which may be available to self-employed or directly-employed home care workers on request.

Service users arranging their own care

Local authorities have been encouraged by the Department of Health to make sure that support is available for those receiving direct payments (see page 53). The National Centre for Independent Living (NCIL) is an advisory body, which is able to give general information to service users about employing their own home care worker, and on organisations that can give advice locally (see Appendix 4 for contact details). Local support groups are growing and can offer information or advice on issues concerning handling money to both service users and their home care workers. Appendix 3 lists some useful publications.

Case study

There had been a problem of theft by a home care worker, and the person concerned was convicted and placed on probation. The local support group used the case to address concerns of service users who employ their own staff about how to handle a situation when a person may have stolen money. It also listed some helpful hints in its newsletter about insurance cover for theft, PIN number safety, checking change and using receipts.

In some cases, it may be helpful to suggest to the service user that they discuss the arrangements being planned with their family or carers to seek their views about whether the safeguards are adequate.

Service users who are employing their own staff should be encouraged to take up written references of the person they plan to employ. They should also draw up a written contract so that both parties are clear about the conditions of service. It may be useful for both parties to check their insurance cover for any liabilities in respect of injury and the handling of money or goods (see page 95).

Most people use their own money to pay for the private home care worker. However, some people receive state support (the Independent Living Fund or direct payments from the local authority) in order to pay for the care they need, either from a home care agency or to employ their own home care workers. The rules for these payments are explained in the following sections.

Independent Living Funds (ILF)

There are two Independent Living Funds – the Extension Fund and the 1993 Fund. The Extension Fund is for people who were receiving payments prior to April 1993, and the 1993 Fund is for people receiving payments since that time. Prior to April 1993, people aged over 66 were able to apply. Since that date, payments from the ILF have been limited to those who *apply* before their 66th birthday, although payments continue once they reach that age.

Both ILF funds make cash payments to enable people to pay for their home care worker. They are government funded, but are run independently by a Board of Trustees. The person is informed of the amount awarded and payments will start once the Fund has received details of who the home care worker(s) will be and how much each will be paid. The payment is made net of any contribution that the service user has to make out of their income. Since April 2002, a service user's earnings are disregarded in the calculation of any contributions.

New applicants are only eligible for the 1993 Fund. Under this Fund, joint care packages, which are a combination of services or direct payments from the local authority and cash from the Fund, are agreed. To receive a payment, the person has to fulfil the following conditions:

- be severely disabled and need help with personal care or household duties to maintain an independent life;
- be at least 16 and under 66 years old;
- be receiving Disability Living Allowance (Care) at the higher rate (see page 62);
- have an income that does not cover their care costs;
- have less than £18,500 savings;
- be living alone or with people who cannot meet their care needs;
- be likely to need care for at least 6 months.

ⓘ For more information, contact the Independent Living Fund (see Appendix 4 for contact details).

Social services direct payments

Since 1997, local authorities have been allowed to make direct payments to people for care services, which they have assessed the person as needing, rather than providing or arranging it themselves. As long as the care meets the person's assessed needs, service users can choose how they receive it and from whom. They can use their direct payment to arrange their own home care worker privately, or have a combination of services, some privately and others provided by or through the local authority. Direct payments increase service users' choice and give them the opportunity to manage their own care. Informal or family carers can also receive direct payment for services they are assessed as needing.

Not all local authorities run direct payment schemes, although many have been setting them up during 2002. However, by April 2003, local authorities will have to start offering service users the option of a direct payment, if the person meets the qualification criteria.

There are national criteria for receiving a direct payment. The person must:

- be assessed as needing services in their own right;
- be aged 16 or over;
- be willing to have payments;
- be able to manage payments (alone or with assistance);
- not be subject to certain mental health or criminal justice legislation.

There are some restrictions on who can be employed using the direct payment – they cannot be used to pay a spouse or partner, or a close relative living in the same household. Even though the service user receives money rather than services, they are subject to the same rules as the local authority for charging for home care services (see Chapter 9).

ⓘ For more details on direct payments, see Age Concern Factsheet 24 *Direct Payments from social services*.

KEY POINTS FROM THIS CHAPTER

Do:

- follow the principles of confidentiality and respect service users' choices when handling money;
- set ground rules and agree them in writing;
- help the service user understand the need for agreements;
- use the experience of local authorities and agencies;
- inform older people, who want to arrange their own services, about the possibility of direct payments.

Don't:

- just handle money and rely on trust;
- ignore information and procedures that are available on handling money.

4 Helping service users with their finances

People who use home care services have widely varying sources and levels of income and capital. Their knowledge of benefits, and their ability to budget, may also vary. This chapter explores some of the financial issues on which a service user might ask a home care worker for information or advice. Home care workers should never give specific advice to a service user on their individual finances, but they are in a position to provide information to enable service users to make more informed choices, or to get expert advice, if this is needed.

This chapter outlines the following benefits to which a service user may be entitled:

- Attendance Allowance (see page 60);
- Disability Living Allowance (see page 62);
- Invalid Care Allowance/Carers Allowance (see page 63);
- Means-tested benefits:
  - Income Support/Minimum Income Guarantee (see page 64);
  - Housing Benefit (see page 64);
  - Council Tax Benefit (see page 64);
  - Pension Credit (due October 2003) (see page 68);
  - Supporting People Services (due April 2003) (see page 68);
- Other financial benefits:
  - help with Council Tax (see page 69);
  - help with fuel costs (see page 69);
  - help with heating, insulation and draught proofing (see page 69);
  - help with repairs and improvements (see page 70);
  - help from the Social Fund (see page 70);

- help with health costs (see page 71);
- help for people with industrial injuries or who were injured in the forces or during the Second World War (see page 72).

The chapter starts, however, by looking at what help or advice a home care worker may be able to give about benefits, and then covers ways of helping with budgeting and obtaining financial advice. As well as welfare benefits, home care workers might find it useful to know who can get payments from the Independent Living Funds or direct payments from social services (see Chapter 3).

Helping with welfare benefits

It is vital that service users are aware of the benefits they can claim. Whilst the vast majority receive their state pension without any difficulty, there are other, more complicated benefits that can be missed by people who would be entitled to them. The Department for Work and Pensions (DWP), formerly the Department of Social Security (DSS), gives estimates of underclaimed benefits. The figures for 1999/2000 show that between 390,000 and 770,000 pensioners failed to claim Income Support (now called the Minimum Income Guarantee – MIG – for people aged 60 or over). A DSS survey in 1997 suggested that only 40 to 60 per cent of those entitled to Attendance Allowance were claiming it.

Local authorities are aware that many service users do not realise that they might be entitled to benefits, and many already run specific campaigns to help service users claim benefits. From April 2003, local authorities have to give benefits advice when they are charging for home care services (see Chapter 9). As most local authorities charge for their services, the majority of service users, provided with care via social services, will receive benefits advice at the time their charge is worked out.

The role of home care workers

Home care workers can play a vital role in encouraging service users to claim benefits. They may be the first person to pick up that a service user's condition has deteriorated, so that someone getting the daytime rate of Attendance Allowance, for example, might now qualify for the higher rate for night-time. Home care workers who can explain a particular benefit, or provide a relevant leaflet, can sometimes help service users in their decision to claim. Home care workers may also be able to arrange help for the service user to fill out their claim form, if the service user is unable to complete it themselves.

It may be that home care workers will have a less important role in giving benefits information for local authority service users, once local authorities are required to give benefits advice as part of their charging policy, from April 2003 (see page 127). However, other service users may still find such information of value, and even local authority service users may be helped if their home care worker is able to pick up that a benefit might be claimed because of a change in their circumstances.

Case study

Mrs Da Vita had a full benefits check when she started to receive her home care service and, as a result, she was able to claim a number of benefits. Three months later, when the stairs were becoming increasingly difficult for her to manage, she decided to move her bed downstairs and turn her sitting room into a bedroom. Her husband continued to sleep upstairs in the bedroom. Her home care worker, Claire, thought that it might be possible to get a reduction in her Council Tax if a living room had been turned into a bedroom. She checked this out with a local benefits adviser and was informed that this was correct. She suggested to Mrs Da Vita that she might want to apply to the council for the Disability Reduction Scheme (see page 69). As a result, her home, which had been in band D, was re-assessed for Council Tax at band C.

Home care workers should be clear about the level of involvement that is expected of them in claiming benefits. If this includes help with filling out claim forms, it is essential that they receive adequate training about the benefits, the time limits for claiming and appeals, and who can give further advice, if needed.

Even if home care workers are not expected to help with individual claims, it is very useful if they have a basic knowledge of benefits that service users could claim, and the particular problems that may cause underclaiming. It is important to know about up-to-date leaflets that explain the benefits clearly, either produced by the Department for Work and Pensions (DWP) or by other organisations locally, and to have contacts with local specialist benefits advice agencies.

Some of the most common reasons for not claiming benefits are:

- *Lack of awareness of the benefit.* This is very common and, in spite of all the information produced, it is surprising how many older people have not heard of Attendance Allowance or know about Council Tax Benefit.
- *Misunderstanding the rules.* Many people who live alone often do not think they can claim Attendance Allowance, either because they think that they have too much money in savings to claim, or because they do not get much help. It is based on the *need* for help, not how much help a person actually receives. Another common fear is that, if they get Attendance Allowance, it will be taken off their Income Support/MIG. In reality, it may *increase* the amount of Income Support/MIG, Housing Benefit or Council Tax Benefit (see page 66 for details of how means-tested benefits can be increased by the receipt of Attendance Allowance).
- *Having been turned down in the past.* Service users may be reluctant to go through the claims process again if they have been turned down in the past. In the case of Attendance Allowance, however, it may be that their condition has worsened and they now fulfil the disability conditions. It may also be that some benefits rules have changed. For example, for Income Support/MIG the capital rules increased to £12,000 for people aged 60 or over in 2001, which meant more people qualified. There will be further major changes in October 2003, when the Government introduces a new benefit called the Pension Credit (see page 68). It is expected that many more pensioners will become entitled to benefit.
- *Not wanting to claim.* Some service users may still not wish to claim benefits, even though they have the information and a claim is likely to succeed. It is important to try to establish the reason for

not claiming, and to point out the advantages of claiming. If the service user does not wish to claim, however, it is their choice and they should not be forced into a claim they do not want to make. However, support and encouragement may help overcome any reluctance to claim.

Home care workers should never tell a service user that they will or will not be entitled to a benefit. It is up to the officers administering the benefits to make a decision on the facts presented to them. Home care workers and service users should seek advice from those who specialise in benefits or benefits advice, if they are unsure whether to claim.

Helping with budgeting

Shopping or paying bills on a service user's behalf may involve the home care worker in aspects of budgeting. Such help should be limited to the extent of discussing special offers in the shops or making suggestions on which items to purchase, particularly if the service user has not had recent experience of shopping. Similarly, the home care worker could help the service user explore new ways of paying bills or spreading the cost.

When a service user is having problems with budgeting, home care workers should encourage them to seek expert advice. Citizens Advice Bureaux (CABx) and some local authorities have money or debt advisers who can help with prioritising the bills and, if necessary, negotiate with companies with whom debts have built up. Home care workers should not negotiate on behalf of service users, unless it is a specific part of their job for which they have been trained.

If a service user has become confused about budgeting and, because of this, their payment of bills has become erratic, home care workers need to be alert to the possibility of more formal arrangements being made through appointeeship, registering an enduring power of attorney or receivership (see Chapter 5). If a member of the service user's family takes on this role, home care workers may be able to provide information on the specialist advice agencies in the area, especially if the service user's finances have become muddled and debts have built up.

If a service user wants advice from a home care worker about the best way to invest their money, or decisions about their property, they should be made aware of the need to seek independent advice from a registered financial adviser. The Financial Services Authority regulates financial businesses. Home care workers should never give financial advice, or recommend a particular adviser. Lists of independent financial advisers can be found in the Yellow Pages. Most banks and building societies can only advise on their own products.

ℹ️ For more details, see Age Concern Information sheet LC/4 *How to get information and advice about your investments.*

Further information on benefits

This section gives brief details of benefits to which service users might be entitled, and examples of how information can help them to make a claim. However, whilst many of the basic rules may remain the same for some time, others will change, as will the figures quoted. It is essential that service users, or home care worker who are encouraging service users to claim benefits, have up-to-date information. This section should always be used, therefore, with the benefits handbooks, *Paying for Care* and *Disability Rights Handbook* (see Appendix 3) or the Age Concern Factsheets listed, as these are updated each year. National organisations and local councils also produce regular, up-to-date information.

Attendance Allowance

This is a non 'means-tested' benefit for people aged 65 or over. It does not matter, therefore, how much money the person has, as it is based purely on what help they need. It is paid at two rates: one for people who need help during the day; and a higher rate for those who need help both day and night. The type of help needed has to be either:

- 'attention' – connected with 'bodily functions' such as eating, getting dressed, going to the toilet or washing. It includes activities when help or guidance is needed such as reading out the labels on tins due to visual impairment, or helping someone with a hearing impairment understand a conversation; or

- 'supervision' – to make sure the older person is not putting themselves or others in danger. The supervision test includes the risk of falls.

The need for 'attention' has to be frequent throughout the day (more than just once or twice), or for prolonged (more than 20 minutes) or repeated (two times or more) periods at night. The need for 'supervision' has to be continual (but not non-stop) during the day, or another person needs to be awake for prolonged periods or at frequent intervals (at least three times) to watch over the person. The person must have needed the attention or supervision for six months, unless they are terminally ill (see 'special rules' on page 62).

It is important for service users, and whoever helps fill in the claim form, to understand that it is the *need* for attention or supervision that has to be shown, not whether they actually get it. Service users who live alone often assume that they will not qualify as they do not have someone with them all the time or, indeed, may only see their home care worker a few days a week.

If the person performs the tasks themselves because there is no one to help them, they will need to explain all the difficulties they have. If they have had falls or dizzy spells, it is important these are all listed (along with any injury the person may have suffered) on the claim form, even if there was no one around to help them at the time.

Some older people worry that, if they explain all the difficulties they have on the Attendance Allowance form, they will be told they will have to go into a care home. Home care workers may need to explain that it is not the officials who deal with this claim who make any decisions about where a person should live, and that the information they give is confidential. Some older people also worry that, if they fill in an Attendance Allowance claim form, they might lose Income Support/MIG. However, this should not happen – in fact, it might *increase* their Income Support/MIG (see page 66).

The form is long, and asks very personal questions, and so can be a daunting task even when the older person gets help. It concentrates on what the person *can't* do rather than all the things they can do. The home care worker needs to be sensitive to this if they know that the person is making a claim for Attendance Allowance.

If the home care worker has been trained in benefits, they may be able to help the service user work out what difficulties they have which should be stressed on the claim form. Alternatively, the home care worker could contact an agency that specialises in benefits to get advice about filling in the claim form.

Special rules for terminal illness: if a service user is terminally ill (they have a progressive illness that could limit their life expectancy to six months or less), they will qualify for the higher rate of Attendance Allowance immediately, even if they do not need help. It is possible for someone to receive Attendance Allowance under 'special rules' without knowing their prognosis. The service user, or someone claiming on their behalf, needs to tick the 'special rules' box on the claim form and the doctor has to send in a special form to explain the person's condition.

It is vital that home care workers use a great deal of tact and do not act alone in situations when it is not clear if the service user or the family are aware of how ill the person is, or that they may not have long to live. If the service user does not get Attendance Allowance, or only gets the lower rate, it may be necessary to liaise with the service user's care manager, or specialist nurses who may be visiting, to see if they are raising the possibility of a claim with the service user or their family.

Disability Living Allowance

This is a benefit with many of the same rules as Attendance Allowance but it is for people who are under 65 years old when they claim. There are three main differences to Attendance Allowance:

- there is a 'care component' which includes a lower level of payment for personal care, in addition to the two rates paid at the same level as Attendance Allowance. This lower rate is for people who need help for a 'significant portion' of the day, often with getting up or going to bed, or for those who cannot prepare a main meal for themselves. The two higher rates have the same rules as Attendance Allowance, as outlined in the previous section.

- there is a 'mobility component' which is not available to people who become disabled after the age of 65. There are two levels of payment: a lower amount, if the person can walk but needs someone with them for guidance or supervision; and a higher amount for those who are unable to walk, or have great difficulty in walking because of a physical disability, or because of severe behavioural problems.
- the claimant only has to have needed the help or had difficulty in walking for three months, but must expect to satisfy the rules for the next six months.

It is important for home care workers, who are working with anyone aged under 65, to be aware that the possibility of claiming the lower rate for care or for help towards mobility will be lost if the person does not claim the Disability Living Allowance before their 65th birthday. It does not matter if their condition has not lasted for three months by the time they reach the age of 65; the benefit can be paid as long as the disability started and the claim is made before they are 65 years old. Once a person gets Disability Living Allowance, it will continue after the age of 65. This is why some older people get help with mobility and/or their benefit is called Disability Living Allowance rather than Attendance Allowance.

i For more details on Attendance Allowance and Disability Living Allowance see Age Concern Factsheet 34 *Attendance Allowance and Disability Living Allowance.*

Invalid Care Allowance/Carers Allowance

Invalid Care Allowance (ICA) will change its name to Carers Allowance in April 2003. It is paid to informal or family carers who spend at least 35 hours a week caring for someone who receives Attendance Allowance or Disability Living Allowance (Care) at one of the two higher rates (see page 62). It does not apply to paid carers. If a carer works, in addition to the 35 hours a week caring, they lose ICA if they earn more than £77 a week (2003/2004).

New rules introduced from October 2002 mean that, for the first time, people aged 65 or over are able to claim ICA. This may not make much difference financially because, if the claimant is receiving a state retirement pension, this will reduce or cancel out any ICA awarded. The change may help those who do not receive a state retirement pension or receive a lower rate, as their pension and ICA together will be brought up to the level of ICA (£43.15 per week in 2003/2004). However, even if it is not paid, being entitled to ICA will mean that the Carer Premium will be included in means-tested benefits calculation. If the person they care for receives a means-tested benefit, however, they may need to seek benefits advice before they claim, as claiming ICA can affect the levels of means-tested benefits paid to the person being cared for (see page 65).

ⓘ For more details, see Age Concern Information sheet LC/15 *Invalid Care Allowance – changes in October 2002*, or contact Carers UK (see Appendix 4 for contact details).

Means-tested benefits

Payment of means-tested benefits is dependent on a person's capital (savings) and income. *Income Support* is a benefit to cover general living costs, renamed the *Minimum Income Guarantee* (*MIG*) for people aged 60 or over, and generally referred to in this book as Income Support/MIG. *Housing Benefit* and *Council Tax Benefit* are, as their names suggest, specific benefits to help towards rent and Council Tax.

The rules for these means-tested benefits are mostly the same, although Income Support/MIG is only paid if the person has capital of no more than £8,000 for those aged under 60, £12,000 for those aged 60 or over, and £16,000 if the person is permanently in a care home. Housing Benefit and Council Tax Benefit are payable if a person has capital of no more than £16,000. In all these benefits, any capital of over £3,000 (under 60), £6,000 (60 or over) and £10,000 (in a care home) attracts what is called tariff income of £1 for every £250 (or part thereof) above that amount.

Each year the Government sets the minimum levels that a person needs to live on. For older people this is made up of:

- a *Personal Allowance*; and
- a *Pensioner Premium* for people aged 60 or over.

This amount combined is used to bring a person's income up to the Minimum Income Guarantee.

A further amount, the *Severe Disability Premium*, can be added to the calculation, if the person receives Attendance Allowance – or either of the equivalent rates of Disability Living Allowance (Care) – and either lives alone or with someone who is registered blind or who also receives Attendance Allowance or Disability Living Allowance (Care). People are still regarded as living alone, in some circumstances, if they jointly own or rent the property in which they live. If any person looking after them receives Invalid Care Allowance (called Carers Allowance from April 2003), the Severe Disability Premium is not paid.

Other premiums can be paid: for example, a *Family Premium* for those with children; a *Disability Premium* for people who are disabled and aged under 60; and an *Enhanced Disability Premium* for people aged under 60 who get the highest rate of Disability Living Allowance (Care). There is also a *Carer Premium* for people who are *entitled* to Invalid Care Allowance/Carers Allowance (even if it is not paid because they get another benefit which is paid at a higher rate).

The premiums a person qualifies for are added together to form the 'applicable amount', and the amount of benefit paid will top up a person's income to this level. Most of that income is taken into account and taken away from the applicable amount to give the amount of benefit (*but Attendance Allowance and Disability Living Allowance are ignored*). The person will not be entitled to Income Support/MIG if their weekly income is more than the applicable amount. If it is less, the difference will be the amount of Income Support/MIG that is paid. However, even if a person's income is higher than the applicable amount, they might still be able to get Housing Benefit (if they pay rent) or Council Tax Benefit, as this is worked out on a sliding scale.

i For more details about means-tested benefits, see Age Concern Factsheet 25 *Income Support (Minimum Income Guarantee) and the Social Fund* and Factsheet 17 *Housing Benefit and Council Tax Benefit.*

INCOME SUPPORT/MIG AND ATTENDANCE ALLOWANCE

It is always worth considering claiming Income Support/MIG if the service user:

- is aged 60 or over and has no more than £12,000 savings, and particularly so if they start to receive Attendance Allowance; or
- is aged under 60, if they have no more than £8,000 in savings and get Disability Living Allowance (Care) at one of the two higher rates. Many people do not realise that when they get Attendance Allowance/Disability Living Allowance (Care), they *may* be entitled to an *increase* of Income Support/MIG, Housing Benefit or Council Tax Benefit due to the Severe Disability Premium. However, unless they tell the relevant agencies that they now get Attendance Allowance/Disability Living Allowance (Care) and make a claim for the means-tested benefit, if they have not been entitled before, they could miss out on that benefit.

It is very difficult to get means-tested benefits backdated. Benefits advice agencies often suggest, therefore, that the person completes the forms for means-tested benefits at the same time as they apply for Attendance Allowance/Disability Living Allowance. Even though they may not qualify for a means-tested benefit until the Attendance Allowance/Disability Living Allowance (Care) claim has been sorted out, the means-tested benefit should be backdated to the original claim.

Even people who have been receiving Attendance Allowance, or the equivalent Disability Living Allowance (Care), may have missed putting in a claim for the means-tested benefits, or they may not be getting the correct level of benefit, if the relevant agencies are not aware that the person now qualifies. Because the rules for the Severe Disability Premium are quite complex, it is not unknown for it to be missed out in the Income Support/MIG calculation.

Case study

Mr and Mrs Bough live in sheltered accommodation. Mr Bough had been receiving Attendance Allowance for a number of years as he suffers from Alzheimer's disease. Mrs Sidu, the manager of the accommodation scheme, had helped Mrs Bough put in a claim for Invalid Care Allowance (ICA) when it was extended to people over 65 in October 2002. Mrs Bough did not get the benefit as her pension was higher than ICA, but it did mean that their Income Support/MIG was increased by the current rate of the Carer Premium.

Mrs Bough, in spite of caring for her husband, suffered from arthritis and asthma, which was gradually getting worse. Mrs Sidu wondered if Mrs Bough should now make a claim for Attendance Allowance. Mrs Bough was sceptical as she could not see how she could get Attendance Allowance when she was caring for her husband and was worried that they might lose the Carer Premium. Mrs Sidu took advice from the Welfare Rights Unit, and it was explained that if Mrs Bough was caring for her husband for 35 hours a week, she would still be considered a carer and the Carer Premium would not be affected. In addition, if Mrs Bough got the Attendance Allowance, both she and her husband would qualify for the Severe Disability Premium in their Income Support/MIG.

Mrs Sidu helped Mrs Bough fill in the claim form for Attendance Allowance, being careful to stress the difficulties she had in dressing and washing, and that she had had falls and needed help when she had asthma attacks. Attendance Allowance was granted. Mrs Sidu explained that it was important to tell the local social security office that both she and her husband now got Attendance Allowance as they would each get the Severe Disability Premium added into their Income Support/MIG calculation. A few weeks later this was confirmed and their income increased by a total of over £100 a week.

Pension Credit and Supporting People Services

The rules for financial support are always subject to change. Two new systems due to be introduced are the Pension Credit (October 2003), and Supporting People Services (April 2003).

- *Pension Credit* – a new type of benefit in two parts. For people aged 60 or over there will be a 'guaranteed income top-up' which will work in the same way as the current Income Support/MIG. There is also a 'savings credit' for people aged 65 or over, providing extra cash for people who have some savings or have put money into a second pension. Savings of up to £6,000 will be ignored, but there will be no upper savings limit, and the amount of tariff income (see page 64) calculated from capital over £6,000 will be less. This and the savings credit will enable many older people, who have not qualified for help in the past, to claim this additional benefit. Although the Pension Credit is likely to be advertised when it is introduced, older people may still not be aware that they might qualify for a means-tested benefit. Home care workers could use any advertising material to draw it to the attention of service users they visit.

  ℹ For further details, see Age Concern Factsheet 48 *Pension Credit* or Age Concern Information sheet LC/14 *The Pension Credit – questions and answers.*

- *Supporting People Services* – rents for sheltered housing currently include the costs of service charges (such as the warden support), which are met through Housing Benefit (or through Income Support/MIG for owner-occupiers). From April 2003, these services will be separated from the rent and met through Supporting People Services. The services will be funded from a special 'pot' of funds held by local authorities. See Chapter 9 for more detail about how these services will be charged.

Other financial benefits

There are a number of other benefits which home care workers should be aware of in order to be able to point the service user towards them. Listed below are some of the more common benefits that service users may be entitled to claim:

Help with Council Tax: in addition to Council Tax Benefit, which is means-tested, there are two other forms of help with Council Tax that are not means-tested. The ***Disability Reduction Scheme*** means Council Tax can be reduced if the service user is disabled and needs extra space for a wheelchair, or needs a living room predominantly for themselves (for example, has a bed in a downstairs room), or has a second bathroom or kitchen. The reduction is in the form of taking the house down a band for Council Tax (for those with houses in Band A, the bill is reduced by 1/6th). There are also ***Council Tax Discounts*** for those who live alone and, in certain circumstances, for those living with carers.

ⓘ For further details, see Age Concern Factsheet 21 *The Council Tax and older people.*

Help with fuel costs: there are ***Winter Fuel Payments*** for most people aged 60 or over, which they should receive automatically. Since its introduction, the rules and the amount have changed on a yearly basis, so it is important to check the levels – it is currently £200 per household. In addition, ***Cold Weather Payments*** are paid to people whose Income Support/MIG includes a Pensioner Premium or Disability Premium (for people with disabilities aged under 60). A payment of £8.50 is made when the daily temperature has been recorded as, or is forecast to be, below 0 degrees Celsius over seven days. These payments should also be automatic.

ⓘ For further details, see Age Concern Factsheet 1 *Help with heating.*

Help with heating, insulation and draught proofing: *Warm Front Grants* (previously known as the Home Energy Efficiency Scheme) offer help with heating and insulation measures, which are specifically tailored to meet the needs of a person's property. There are two levels of grants:

• up to £1,500 for a range of heating improvements and insulation measures, including loft and cavity wall insulation and draught-proofing for households in receipt of certain means-tested or disability benefits.

- up to £2,500 for householders aged 60 or over who are on a mean-tested benefit. This is known as Warm Front Plus. This is to provide insulation measures and, where appropriate, high level efficiency central heating systems for the main living areas. It also provides for security measures in designated high crime areas (see Chapter 6).

i For further details, see Age Concern Factsheet 1 *Help with heating.*

Help with repairs and improvements: in England and Wales, the housing grants system is being changed. The rules are different in Scotland. Currently, private tenants might get a *Renovation Grant* for large-scale repairs or *Home Repair Assistance* towards the costs of certain repairs such as installing an inside toilet, rewiring or minor adaptations up to £5,000. However, under a new regulatory order, local authorities have a new general power to help improve living conditions, which can include adaptations or improvements to a person's home by providing a grant, a loan, materials or any form of assistance. This will replace the current Renovation Grant and Home Repair Assistance by July 2003. The local authority must publish what assistance it is prepared to provide and in what circumstances. As well as discretionary help, there are also mandatory *Disabled Facilities Grants* that cover the cost of work on a variety of improvements or adaptations to make life easier for a person with a disability. They are subject to an assessment of income and savings. They are used when the adaptations are needed to help a disabled person get in and out of the home, or use a bathroom, toilet or kitchen, or improve or provide a suitable heating system.

i For further details, see Age Concern Factsheet 13 *Older home owners: financial help with repairs and adaptations.*

Help from the Social Fund: service users in receipt of Income Support/MIG may be able to get help from the Social Fund with either a *Community Care Grant* or a *Budgeting Loan.* Unlike any other aspect of the social security system, these are discretionary and made from a fixed budget. In addition to being on Income Support/MIG, if the service user has capital of over £1,000 (£500 for those aged under

60), the grant or loan will be reduced pound for pound. Grants do not have to be repaid and are mainly for help to remain in the community (minor repairs, bedding and essential furniture or removal costs); easing exceptional pressures caused by disability or chronic sickness; or help with travel expenses such as attending a funeral or visiting someone who is ill. Loans can be made for similar reasons but have to be repaid. There are also **Crisis Loans**, which can be paid if money is needed urgently in an emergency, or because of a disaster such as a fire or flood, even if the person is not on Income Support/MIG. All savings and income are taken into account and help is only given if it is deemed to be the only way of preventing serious damage or risk to the person's health or safety.

The advantages of applying for a grant rather than a loan should be made clear to the service user. As it is discretionary, it is important to give as much detail as possible about the health of the service user and why it is essential to have the items being requested. It may be helpful to have a letter of support from a GP or care manager.

ⓘ For further details, see Age Concern Factsheet 25 *Income Support (Minimum Income Guarantee) and the Social Fund.*

Help with health costs: people who receive Income Support/MIG are given full help with the following health costs:

- prescriptions;
- dental care;
- sight tests and help with the cost of glasses;
- elastic support stockings, wigs and fabric supports;
- travel costs to hospital.

People not receiving Income Support/MIG may still be able to get some help on the grounds of 'low income' if they have no more than £12,000 savings (£8,000 if aged under 60). (The rules may change when Pension Credit starts in October 2003.) Prescriptions, sight tests and elastic support stockings are all free for everyone aged 60 or over. In addition, some younger people qualify for free prescriptions if they have certain conditions or are unable to get out of the house without the assistance of another person.

If a service user is applying on the grounds of low income, even if they do not need help at the time, it is worth suggesting that they apply for a certificate – for people aged over 60, these are certificates HC2 (for people entitled to full help) and HC3 (for people entitled to partial help). They usually last for 12 months and then have to be renewed. Although it may not seem worth renewing it until needed, it is much easier if the person already has a certificate before they have any treatment, buy new glasses or have to go to hospital. Although refunds are possible, it is sometimes difficult to get them, and involves extra paperwork for the service user.

ⓘ   For further details, see Department of Health leaflet HC11 *Help with health costs.*

Help for people with industrial injuries or who were injured in the forces or during the Second World War: some people who have had accidents at work or have contracted illnesses through the type of work they were doing may be entitled to *Industrial Injury Benefit.* Others who may have been injured or contracted an illness during their time in the forces, either in war or peacetime, may be entitled to a *War Pension.* Injuries and illnesses can include psychological conditions such as schizophrenia and post-traumatic stress disorder. Civilians who were physically injured in the Second World War, either by enemy action or action combating the enemy (such as an injury from making bombs or airplanes), can also claim a war pension. For both Industrial Injury Benefit and War Pensions, there has to be a link with the condition the person now has and the person's previous work or armed service, or what happened to them during the Second World War.

Many people do not make that link themselves or may have claimed in the past and been turned down, or have received benefit for a while, then improved, but now that condition has got worse or a new condition started but which is linked to their old condition. It is always worth asking the person if anything they are now suffering from is linked in any way to the work they used to do or when they were in the forces. If they think it is, expert advice may be useful. Trade unions often have good knowledge about industrial diseases, and the British Legion has expert knowledge on War Pensions. Benefits specialists such as Citizen's Advice Bureaux (CABx) or Welfare Rights services may be able to help or put the person in touch with a specialist adviser. If the claim is being made some years after the event, it can take a long time to sort out (even several years in some cases) but, if it is successful, the level of benefit should compensate for the delay.

Case study

Home care worker, Alun Brown, helps Mr Hughes, aged 81, out of bed and get dressed each day. Mr Hughes has spondylitis. One day, Alun made a chance remark about the cold and damp, which prompted Mr Hughes to talk about the times he had had to wait in the cold and damp on airfields during the war when he was in the RAF. Mr Hughes rarely talked about the war as he did not think his role had been very glamorous. He had been stationed in England in the RAF ambulance service. Most of the time he had spent waiting around in the cold and damp and, once the flights came in, had to help the injured airmen onto stretchers and get them to hospital. He had had treatment on his back during the war, and was told it was spondylitis. He was given a desk job towards the end of the war. For many years, he had no problems with his back until, when he got older, he was again diagnosed as having spondylitis. Alun asked him if he thought that it was due to the war that he now had a back problem. Mr Hughes was sure that it was but had not thought he could make a claim after such a long time as it would be put down to old age. Alun said it may be worth looking into and suggested that Mr Hughes should contact the British Legion. He did and a claim was made. It was clear from the medical records that his condition was linked to his war service, so he was awarded a War Pension in spite of it being over 55 years since the war ended.

KEY POINTS FROM THIS CHAPTER

Do:

- know how far you are expected to be involved in benefit issues;
- make sure you know where to get specialist benefits advice;
- help with benefits claims, if you have had training;
- always suggest a benefit, if the service user might qualify;
- remember it is the service user's choice whether or not to claim;
- know about where service users can obtain independent financial advice.

Don't:

- think you must have *specialist* knowledge about benefits;
- ignore the fact that there are specialist advisers;
- feel that you have to help with claims, if you are uncertain about the rules of the benefit;
- say that a service user will or will not qualify – it is for the officials who process claims to decide;
- pressure a service user into claiming a benefit;
- give financial advice.

5 Helping service users who are unable to manage their financial affairs

This chapter explores the situations that can arise when a person is unable to manage their own financial affairs because they lack the mental capacity to do so. It looks firstly at mental capacity, and the processes that should be followed when assessing a person's capacity to manage their own financial affairs. It then explains briefly the legal procedures that can be put into place (in England and Wales only) to enable someone to act on that person's behalf in relation to their finances, and explains when home care workers themselves might become an appointee. Finally, it looks at how home care workers should work with those who have taken on the responsibility for the service user's finances.

Very few home care workers will act on behalf of the service user. It is essential, however, that they have a good understanding of the legal implications of the powers that are available to others to manage a person's financial affairs. Home care workers should also be aware when the use of such powers may be appropriate.

There are three ways of managing people's finances if they are no longer capable of doing so themselves, which are explained briefly in this chapter:

- a registered enduring power of attorney;
- appointeeship for state benefits;
- receivership under the Court of Protection.

General decision making and protection

The question of decision making and of protection for those who lack mental capacity is currently the subject of debate. The present legislation is widely considered to be inadequate. The Government has introduced a White Paper, *Making Decisions*, which proposes a number of changes to the law to offer more adequate protection to those who lack mental capacity, but it is not yet clear when the law will be changed. However, one important proposal would enable people to choose in advance, before they lose capacity, who they would like to make decisions about their health and social welfare, *as well as* their financial affairs. Currently, in England and Wales, a person can select an attorney for their financial affairs only, and not for making decisions about their health treatment or support services. The situation is different in Scotland, where these provisions are already in place.

All the arrangements described in this chapter give another person the responsibility for dealing only with the person's finances *not* for any other decisions.

Deciding whether someone is capable of managing their own financial affairs

It is a key principle that people should be assumed to have mental capacity unless it is demonstrated otherwise. There is no clear-cut definition of 'mental incapacity'. Some people may make seemingly bizarre choices about how they spend their money, but may not be incapable of managing their own affairs. Others may have a fluctuating condition and be able to understand and manage much better on some days than others.

A person might become increasingly forgetful about where they have put their money, or start hiding it and then be convinced that they have been burgled. They may no longer recognise coins or notes. People who previously paid bills promptly may start to run up debts. However, it is important for home care workers to realise that sometimes medication or a physical condition (such as pneumonia, constipation, heart disease, or urinary or bowel infection) can cause or exacerbate the appearance of confusion, and that these are usually treatable.

It will often be the home care worker who becomes aware of a deteriorating condition which gives rise to concern about mental capacity. It is important not to assume, however, that a person is unable to manage their financial affairs just because they can no longer manage some other aspects of their life. The key question is whether the person has the ability to understand their actions when making a particular decision.

Both managerial staff and those working with service users in their homes should have training and guidance on how financial competence might be assessed and how this relates to mental incapacity. Home care workers should have clear guidance on when to bring their concerns to the attention of their manager, even when this might override the wishes of the service user. Great care is needed, as actions taken can result in the individual losing all control over their finances.

Procedures should establish who is responsible for ensuring that any necessary steps are taken to assess the person's capacity. Relatives should be alerted and consulted, where appropriate. Relatives may also require help themselves in understanding at what point an older person may need to have arrangements made to deal with their financial affairs. Equally, they may need support in allowing the person to make choices and take some risks in spending their money, in spite of the fact that the service user is no longer able to manage all of their financial affairs.

Home care providers should only allow their staff to deal with a third party (such as a relative) in relation to the financial matters of a service user if that third party is duly authorised to act on the service user's behalf.

Arrangements which can be made whilst the person is mentally capable

Powers of attorney

Home care workers should be aware of powers of attorney, and be able to pass on information to the service user, if appropriate. There are two types of power of attorney that home care workers are likely to come across in their day-to-day work – an ordinary power of attorney and an enduring power of attorney. Both types can only be made by a person who is capable of understanding what they are doing at the time of completing the documents. Only an enduring power of attorney can continue once the person lacks mental capacity.

ORDINARY POWER OF ATTORNEY

An ordinary power of attorney allows a person (known as the donor) to hand over financial tasks to another person (the attorney). It is often used by people who go abroad for a period of time, or who do not want to handle their affairs any longer. A donor can appoint one person as attorney or several people.

The donor can choose what tasks the attorney is allowed to undertake on their behalf and by what methods, or give a general power. Donors can continue to act for themselves, either on their own or with the attorney as long as they are capable of doing so.

The document granting the attorneyship is a legal document that shows the extent of the powers for the attorney to show to banks, building societies or social security to prove that authorisation has been given for them to act.

ENDURING POWER OF ATTORNEY

The rules relating to an ordinary power of attorney apply equally to an enduring power of attorney (EPA), except that an ordinary power of attorney ceases to have effect if the donor becomes mentally incapacitated. An EPA enables the donor to choose the person who will make financial decisions for them when they are no longer able to make their own decisions.

Donors can appoint someone either:

- to take over their affairs at once (as described above) and continue even after they have become mentally incapable; or
- to only start acting as an attorney once they are no longer able to act for themselves.

It can be cancelled at any time whilst the donor still has the capacity to understand the action being taken.

Local authorities (and agencies providing home care as part of a specialist scheme) do not normally hold a power of attorney, as the donor has to name an individual. Home care workers should not hold an EPA in their working capacity.

Once the donor starts to become mentally incapacitated, the EPA *must* be registered with the Public Guardianship Office (formerly the Public Trust Office). If it is not registered, any actions that are undertaken will be without legal authority. Once it is registered, the original document is stamped as registered and carries a seal. There is a fee for registration. It is advisable for procedures to be in place for home care providers to check the documentation to establish that the EPA has been registered, if they are handling money that is being dealt with by an attorney.

Currently, no medical evidence of the donor's mental incapacity is required when the attorney applies to register with the Public Guardianship Office. It is often difficult, therefore, for attorneys to know when they should be thinking about registering the power. The attorney, who might be a close relative, may have problems facing the fact that the service user is no longer mentally capable.

One drawback of an EPA is that there are currently no routine checks on attorneys made by the Public Guardianship Office. It only becomes involved if concerns have been raised. Although the vast majority of enduring powers of attorney work well, there are also cases of serious financial abuse that have gone undetected.

ℹ️ For further details, see the Public Guardianship Office booklet, *Enduring powers of attorney.*

When to consider a power of attorney

If a service user is considering taking out either power of attorney, it is important that they choose someone they can trust. It is also advisable for them to talk it over with close relatives or friends, or even get legal or independent advice if they have substantial sums of money, either in cash or property, or the proposed attorney could stand to gain.

Case study

Mrs Gibbs has been the home care worker for Mr Prentiss for several years. His daughter, Mrs Archer, has an enduring power of attorney (EPA) and arrangements have been put in place so that money has been left with Mr Prentiss for the weekly shopping. Over the past year, Mr Prentiss has become very forgetful and there have been times when he has not had the money for his shopping. Mrs Gibbs has tended to put this down to his forgetfulness and, when talking to the daughter on the telephone about this, Mrs Archer has promised to get the shopping in herself. Mrs Gibbs has growing concerns about how little Mrs Archer buys and that no effort is made to buy the type of food Mr Prentiss likes.

Mrs Gibbs raises her concerns about Mr Prentiss with her manager and the fact that he no longer seems to be able to manage his money. His care manager is called in to do a reassessment, in the course of which he speaks to Mrs Archer about the need to register the EPA. The GP sees Mr Prentiss and confirms that his memory problems have reached the stage when he can no longer manage his finances. Mrs Archer promises to register the EPA. She also promises to buy more of the food Mr Prentiss likes. It was agreed to review the situation in six months.

Mrs Gibbs remained concerned that the situation did not improve, in spite of repeated discussions with the daughter. Things came to a head when Mr Prentiss's other daughter appeared and was worried about her father. The care manager was concerned to find that this daughter had received no notification of any application for registration of the EPA. Mrs Archer's sister consequently wrote to the Public Guardianship Office, sending in medical evidence of her father's mental incapacity, and expressing concern that the attorney (her sister) had made no attempt to register it. She then applied to become a receiver, as her father was no longer able to cancel the EPA as he lacked capacity. It was discovered that Mrs Archer had transferred about £10,000 into her own account in order to prop up her business, on the grounds that her father would have wanted this. Most of his capital had disappeared since the time Mr Prentiss had become forgetful and was no longer able to control what his daughter was doing.

As Mrs Archer had already used the money, it was impossible to get it back for Mr Prentiss, and her sister was reluctant to take the matter to court. She did agree that her father would probably have left this money to his daughter, but was very upset by the underhand way Mrs Archer had used her position of attorney.

Arrangements for people no longer capable of making financial decisions

Appointeeship for state pensions and benefits

This is one of the most common ways of dealing with the financial affairs of people entitled to a state benefit (such as a pension or a means-tested benefit) who can no longer manage their finances because of mental incapacity. An appointeeship does not give the appointee the right to make decisions about other income such as an occupational pension. Neither can they make decisions about savings, unless those savings are made up of a limited amount of unspent benefits. If the service user has other income or savings, unless an enduring power of attorney has already been drawn up (see page 78), an application will need to be made for receivership, as outlined on page 84.

The Secretary of State for Work and Pensions can appoint someone else, an appointee, to act on the claimant's behalf. The appointee is responsible for:

- claiming any benefits;
- receiving the benefits and spending them on the claimant's behalf;
- informing the Department for Work and Pensions (DWP – formerly the Department of Social Security) of any changes that could affect the benefits of the person for whom they are the appointee;
- asking for a review or appeal, if they are concerned about any aspects of the claim.

Once appointed, the benefits remain in the claimant's name, although they are paid to the appointee. Any money received must be spent on the claimant. However, there are currently no routine checks on appointees. If concerns are raised, the DWP will check how the money is being spent. The appointeeship can be revoked if the appointee is not acting in the interests of the claimant, and someone else can be appointed in their place.

In most cases, relatives or friends act as an appointee, although this role could be taken on by a manager or staff member from the local authority or an independent agency, including the home care worker. Unlike arrangements for powers of attorney (see page 78), an appointeeship can be held by an organisation such as a home care provider agency or a local authority. Some care agencies that run advocacy services or schemes for people with learning disabilities will also take on appointeeship. The organisation is responsible for ensuring that any of their representatives authorised to collect benefit payments are acting in the person's best interests.

WHEN THE HOME CARE WORKER OR MANAGER IS THE APPOINTEE

In most cases, when a local authority or independent service provider has taken on the role of appointee, it will normally be a manager who is appointed. However, home care workers might take on this role occasionally. This situation is more common in independent living schemes such as group homes for people with learning disabilities.

When individual home care workers or managers hold the appointeeship, guidance must be in place to ensure that they are fully aware of their role and responsibilities. Staff will need to have a clear understanding of benefit rules to ensure claims are made at appropriate times and that overpayments do not inadvertently occur. They should inform the DWP of any changes of circumstances. The principles of involving the service user in as many decisions as possible must be followed, as must the requirement to spend the person's money on their behalf. Financial management arrangements should be closely monitored when the appointee is an individual within the organisation, including a regular review of whether appointeeship is still needed.

ARRANGING AN APPOINTEESHIP

Anyone can write to the local social security office and ask for an appointeeship to be made, if they think that a person who is receiving benefits is no longer capable of managing their own affairs. Social security staff should visit the claimant to satisfy themselves that the claimant is not capable of managing their affairs. Where necessary, they may seek medical advice. They will also interview the prospective appointee to explain the responsibilities of an appointee and to ensure that the person is suitable and willing to act.

APPOINTEE OR AGENT?

Home care workers must be aware of the differences between appointeeship and the agent arrangements (see page 38) to collect pensions and other state benefits. The main differences are:

- agents are used when the person is mentally capable of authorising someone to collect their benefits; appointeeship is used when the person is not mentally capable of managing their affairs;
- agents collect benefits and return the money to the service user (unless agreed by the service user that some is used for their shopping); appointees are authorised by the DWP to spend the benefits on the service user's behalf;
- when there is an agent, it is the responsibility of the service user to notify the social security office of any changes of circumstances and to claim benefits; an appointee is responsible for this.

Home care workers should be alert to the fact that, if the person no longer has the capacity to manage their affairs, even though they may still be able to sign the back of their pension order, the agent arrangement is no longer appropriate or valid.

ⓘ For further details, see the Department for Work and Pensions' information leaflet, *A helping hand with benefits: a guide for agents and appointees.*

The Court of Protection

If a person has not set up an enduring power of attorney, and has assets other than from state benefits, receivership powers can be granted by the Court of Protection, which was established to look after and manage the financial affairs of those who cannot manage for themselves due to mental incapacity. The Public Guardianship Office carries out the administration of the Court's decisions.

Before it will become involved, the Court has to be satisfied (with medical evidence) that the person has a mental incapacity that causes their inability to manage their financial affairs. Once this is established, the person then becomes a patient of the Court (the term 'patient' is used in the legislation but the term 'client' is now used more frequently).

The Court of Protection encourages the involvement of the client in their financial affairs. Even when the Court has become involved, it may decide that a person is able to manage some aspects of their financial affairs. The Court may agree to small amounts being held in a bank account for the client to manage themselves.

RECEIVERSHIP

If a person needs help with their financial affairs and they have income other than benefits or have capital (either in savings, shares or in property), an application should be made to the Court of Protection for someone to be appointed as a receiver. Once appointed, they will be responsible for the client's income and pay it into a special bank account opened as a receiver. The Customer Services Unit of the Public Guardianship Office will advise on how to make the application and will assess how much help and supervision will be needed to manage the client's finances before the Court makes an order. When the person's savings are below a certain level (currently £16,000) and their financial affairs are straightforward, the court grants a 'short order', rather than the full receivership.

The receivership order of the Court specifies the powers of the receiver. The Court requires accounts to be submitted and the receiver will need specific authority from the Court before making any transaction that involves capital assets, making loans or gifts, buying or selling property, or taking legal proceedings.

The Court decides who it will appoint as receiver, taking the wishes of the client into account, as far as possible. It will normally be a relative, friend or informal carer. It is highly unlikely that a home care worker would be the receiver for a service user.

If the financial affairs of the client are complicated, a solicitor or accountant may be appointed. In some cases, it may be an officer from the local authority such as the Director of Social Services, Director of Finance, or Chief Executive. They will not have a day-to-day involvement with each individual's finances and will often be the receiver for a number of people in their area.

The day-to-day responsibility is often delegated and should rest with a person who has the time to devote to the individual. It is preferable that the person should not also be involved in collecting charges for care services from the service user. Potential conflicts of interest can occur when an officer from the local authority is the receiver.

ℹ️ For further details, see Public Guardianship Office booklet, *Receivership handbook*.

Home care workers and a 'third party'

When service users are no longer capable of managing their finances, home care workers will have to work with the person who is managing their affairs (a 'third party'). There should be clear arrangements for the home care worker to be given the money needed for the service user on a day-to-day basis, and decisions made about the safekeeping of pension, benefits and bank books. All transactions made on behalf of the service user need to be recorded, checked and signed by the person managing their affairs. Even when the service user may not fully understand the arrangements, they should still be explained in their presence, and the service user involved as much as possible.

The appointee, attorney or receiver is unlikely to be present when the home care worker undertakes the day-to-day transactions for the service user. In some cases, the third party will be very involved in the service user's life; they may have frequent contact with the home care worker to discuss what purchases might be needed, and arrange for money to be available if they cannot undertake the transaction themselves. In other cases, the third party may live many miles away and be unable to visit regularly.

Particular thought needs to be given to the robustness of receipting arrangements and safekeeping of the amounts of money that will be needed on a day-to-day basis. The recording arrangements, which should be part of the provider's procedures, will need to be explained to the third party, and appropriate measures agreed by the manager, home care worker and the person handling the service user's financial affairs.

Enabling choice

Home care workers should involve service users as much as possible in making decisions about how their money is spent and comply with their wishes. Particular care should be taken to find out the likes and dislikes of someone who may be confused or unable to communicate their wishes easily. Discussions need to take place with the appointee, attorney or receiver about the types of things they know the service user enjoys, and whether they used to buy presents and cards for family or friends, for example, so that such practices can continue, if it is believed that the service user would want this.

If the home care worker shops on a regular basis for the service user, it must not be assumed that they should just buy the same items each week, but try to engage the service user in deciding what they might like.

If the third party who manages the service user's money lives some distance away, or is a solicitor, the home care worker might need to establish dialogue about the upkeep of the home or replacing items of clothing or furniture. Wherever possible, it should be the third party who arranges for any expensive items to be bought, in consultation with the service user. Home care workers need to be clear about their level of responsibility. It may be just to alert the person responsible for managing the service user's affairs that an item is needed, or they might help the service user to choose what they want. Sometimes the home care worker might be involved in the actual purchase. If service users are confused or lack mental capacity, care should be taken to avoid large items being delivered when the service user is alone.

Case study

Mr Wright acted as receiver for his mother but lived quite far away. He had a demanding job and normally only got to see his mother briefly about once a month. The home care worker, Mrs Briggs, noticed that Mrs Wright's chair was getting very shabby, the springs were going and it was quite uncomfortable for Mrs Wright to get out of. Mrs Briggs suggested to Mrs Wright that her son could be contacted to make arrangements for a new chair. Mrs Briggs rang Mr Wright to discuss this. He was quite happy for Mrs Briggs to help his mother choose a chair. As Mrs Wright could not get out of the house easily, Mr Wright arranged for some catalogues to be sent from the local furniture stores that he knew his mother had used in the past. Mrs Briggs helped Mrs Wright choose a chair and sent the information off to Mr Wright.

There was a six-week gap before it could be delivered and Mr Wright did not make any exact arrangements for delivery. The firm telephoned Mrs Wright who agreed a delivery date but did not really understand what she was agreeing to. When the firm delivered the chair, she had forgotten all about it and told them she had a perfectly good chair of her own and they must have the wrong address.

The firm had to contact Mr Wright to explain the problem. He spoke to Mrs Briggs and arranged for the chair to be delivered on a day when she would be there. The firm could not give a precise time but Mrs Briggs was quite confident that, if she showed Mrs Wright a picture of the chair she had chosen and kept reminding her that it was being delivered that day, she would remember. She left the picture by the door and Mrs Wright was quite excited about the chair arriving. When her son phoned that evening, she talked of nothing but having a lovely new chair.

i For more details about all the provisions described in this chapter, see Age Concern Factsheet 22 *Legal arrangements for managing financial affairs.*

KEY POINTS FROM THIS CHAPTER

Do:

- assume the service user has mental capacity unless there is evidence to the contrary;
- be aware of the difficulties of assessing mental capacity;
- alert the service user's care manager if there are concerns about increasing forgetfulness or confusion;
- involve the service user as much as possible, even if they cannot make all their own financial decisions;
- find out, preferably from the service user, what they wish to spend their money on and try to be aware of what they enjoyed buying when they were able to make decisions;
- be aware of procedures for working with a third party;
- only work with third parties who have the legal authority to act;
- try to ensure the wishes of the service user are followed;
- be aware of the different arrangements that exist for people who do not have the capacity to manage their financial affairs.

Don't:

- make assumptions about mental incapacity;
- make judgements about what service users buy;
- continue to collect benefits as an agent if there are concerns about the service user's mental capacity to manage their financial affairs;
- make informal arrangements with relatives or friends who have no power to act;
- ignore the wishes of service users if dealing with their finances through an appointee, attorney or receiver.

6 Security and insurance

This chapter looks at security and insurance issues both for the service user and the home care worker. When there are any dealings with financial affairs or belongings, it is vital that these issues are considered. The chapter looks firstly at the security of the service user, and then goes on to consider security and insurance issues for the home care worker who is handling the finances of an individual. It looks finally at the responsibilities of the local authority in circumstances when a service user has to go into hospital and there is no one to safeguard the property.

Security for service users in their home

Most people take sensible measures to keep their property safe such as using locks, bolts, chains and alarms. If service users own the property, security would normally be their responsibility. In rented accommodation, locks and other security devices would probably be the responsibility of the landlord, although it would be wise to check.

There are a number of precautions that home care workers could usefully bring to the attention of their service users. Care needs to be taken, however, not to dwell on security so much as to frighten service users into thinking that they are in constant danger of being burgled. Statistics show that the risk of being burgled is lower when the head of the household is aged 75+ (3.2 per cent) than when the head of household is aged under 25 (12 per cent) (*British Crime Survey 2000*). Nevertheless, fear of crime is generally higher amongst the older population.

Locks, keys and alarms

If a home care worker is concerned about the state of the locks, or the ease of access that could be gained through the windows, this should be brought to the attention of the service user. If a service user opts for a security chain on the door, home care workers should point out the importance of only using it prior to opening the door, as it could otherwise prevent the entry of legitimate key-holders. Some care may be needed in relation to the installation and use of an alarm if the service user is forgetful, or would have difficulty in setting it. Procedures should cover situations when service users have alarms and the home care worker might need to have the alarm code to stop and re-set them if they have been set off accidentally.

Providers of home care should ensure that their home care workers have details of any local schemes that fit locks and security chains, or give advice to disabled or older people about home security. In some areas, police crime prevention officers visit older people in their homes to discuss security measures they can take.

If service users qualify for a Warm Front Plus grant (see page 69), they may also qualify for security measures for their house, as the grant can include free door and window locks, bolts and alarms. To qualify, a person has to be aged 60 or over, receive a means-tested benefit, and live in a designated 'high crime area'. There are 69 local authority areas designated 'high crime areas', and further information can be obtained from the local authority.

KEY-HOLDING

Some service users may not be able to get to the door to let in the home care worker. In some cases, the home care worker may need to become a key-holder. Other alternatives should be explored, including the specially designed secure boxes outside the front door that allow people who know the combination number to open it and get the key.

Home care workers should always discourage service users from hiding the key outside the house.

Home care providers should have procedures in place for when home care workers hold keys on behalf of service users. These should include:

- a leaflet to explain the system to the service user;
- written authorisation to hold keys;
- receipt of acceptance of the key by the home care worker;
- making sure any key tag does not identify the address of the service user in case it is found by anyone outside the agency;
- the key being stored in a safe place;
- arrangements to allow the key to be passed to another home care worker in the event of sickness of the key-holding home care worker, with the written permission of the service user;
- recording the name of the key-holder. In the event of the home care worker leaving or transferring to another service user, the key should be returned immediately to the service user and this recorded. New arrangements may be needed for the service user to pass it on to a new home care worker;
- respecting the privacy of the service user: home care workers should always knock and announce their presence and request permission to enter before doing so, as outlined in Standard 15 of the National Minimum Standards (see Appendix 1).

If the service user has given a key to a trusted neighbour, it should be agreed in writing that the home care worker can collect the key from that person.

Keys should only be held by home care workers as a last resort and not merely as a convenience because the service user takes a long time to get to the door.

Dealing with callers at the door

Home care workers should understand that they are also 'callers at the door' and should always carry their identification with them and show it to any service user to whom they are not well known. Even if the home care worker knows the person (perhaps from having worked with them previously), it should not be assumed that the service user will remember them if some time has passed since the last visit. Home care providers should ensure that staff identification cards show a photograph of the home care worker, their name and employing organisation in large print, the contact number of the organisation, the date of issue and an expiry date which should not exceed 36 months from the date of issue. Standard 15 of the National Minimum Standards (see Appendix 1) also stipulates that cards should be:

- available in large print for people with visual disabilities;
- laminated or otherwise tamper proof;
- renewed and replaced within at least 36 months from the date of issue;
- returned to the organisation when employment ceases.

Home care workers should encourage their service users to always ask to see the identification of anyone who purports to be visiting in an official capacity. If the service user has a security chain, home care workers should encourage the service user to keep it on until the identity card has been checked. Service users should be made aware that those in an official capacity will have identity cards and, if the person calling does not show it, they should not be allowed in. Bogus callers often pose as officials and can be very convincing. If a service user thinks that they have been the victim of a bogus caller, the home care worker should encourage them to call the police. Care providers should alert home care workers if a bogus caller is known to be working in a particular area, so that they can advise service users to take extra care.

Case study

Mrs Jones mentioned to her home care worker, Ms Bright, that she had been visited the previous day by a very nice gentleman from the local authority, who had come round to do a benefits check as part of the social services' take-up campaign. Ms Bright knew about the campaign as it had been in the press a few weeks earlier. She was a bit worried, however, when she realised that Mrs Jones had not been informed in writing that the council worker was coming. She had not asked to see his identification. He had been very official and had helped her fill in the Attendance Allowance form and the Income Support/MIG form. He had implied that the council would recoup the cost of filling in the forms and that he would come back and see her in about six weeks when the money had come through. Ms Bright asked Mrs Jones if she could check if anyone from the council had been sent to see her. When she rang the Welfare Rights Service, the query was linked with a complaint that had been received by them from a sheltered housing manager about a 'Welfare Rights Officer' demanding 50 per cent of the money that had come through from social security. A number of tenants had been visited. No one from the Welfare Rights Service had visited Mrs Jones. As a result, an alert was put out to all the local home care providers to warn older people about this bogus 'officer' and the police were contacted. He was caught several days later. Mrs Jones got the benefit to which she was entitled but was very upset that she had given such intimate details of her life and finances to someone who was bogus.

Local gas, water and electricity companies can arrange a password service for people who have sight problems. The password is chosen by the person and can be quoted by the caller to confirm that they come from the relevant utility company. Home care agencies should set up a similar service or have a special knock in cases when the service user has poor sight, so that the service user can identify that it is their home care worker at the door.

Doorstep salespeople

All householders have rights in relation to doorstep selling and it would be useful if home care workers were made aware of those rights. If a service user has received an unsolicited visit (and this includes visits agreed beforehand with a telesales operator in a telephone call), and has agreed to buy goods worth over £35, the contract can be cancelled within seven days if they decide they do not want it. By law, the seller must give written details of the right to cancel and failure to do this is a criminal offence.

New legal powers have been introduced to give greater protection to consumers from rogue traders called 'Stop Now Orders'. They allow British consumer protection bodies to pursue rogue traders operating both in the UK and abroad by taking out court injunctions to prevent them from breaking the law. Failure to comply with a 'Stop Now Order' will be treated as contempt of court and punishable by an unlimited fine or imprisonment (previously only small fines were imposed, which did not deter traders). 'Stop Now Orders' include doorstep selling, as well as misleading advertising, unfair contract terms and distance selling through phone, fax, mail order or the internet.

Home care workers should encourage service users to think very carefully before buying from or selling to doorstep salespeople. In particular, they should check out any situation in which an unsolicited builder tells the service user that they need home repairs. If a service user does need repairs to their home, local voluntary organisations may be able to offer advice about getting a builder or provide a list of reputable ones. In some areas, there are home improvement agencies (HIAs), which are 'not for profit' organisations that assist vulnerable homeowners or private sector tenants, who are older, disabled or on low incomes to repair, maintain or adapt their home. HIAs operate locally under a variety of names, including Care & Repair and Staying Put. There is also an umbrella organisation, Foundations, for HIAs. See Appendix 4 for contact details.

The local trading standards department can give advice if there is a problem with particular doorstep traders, and may also be able provide assistance with staff training.

i For further details, see the Department of Trade and Industry's leaflet, *Doorstep Selling: A consumer's guide.*

Unsolicited mail and phonecalls

Some service users find unsolicited mail and telephone calls worrying and may feel pressured into responding to them or buying goods they do not want. They may even be led to believe they have won a major prize. It is possible to reduce unsolicited mail or calls by contacting the 'Mail Preference Service' or the 'Telephone Preference Service' (see Appendix 4).

ⓘ For further details on any of the security issues outlined, see Age Concern Factsheet 33 *Crime prevention for older people.*

Security for home care workers

When a home care worker handles money for a service user, consideration must be given to both the safety of the worker and the security of the money or goods that belong to the service user. Home care workers should not be expected to carry around large amounts of service user's money, and home care providers should put in place sensible precautions to avoid risks to home care workers. This may include varying the time of going to the post office or not wearing the agency's uniform when collecting money or shopping. Home care workers, who regularly collect money for service users, should use money-belts rather than carry the money in their handbags. Local crime prevention advice should be sought when setting up measures aimed at protecting workers.

Any loss or damage to a service user's money or goods, whilst under the responsibility of a home care worker, must be written in the usual visit record and reported to the line manager. Appropriate agencies such as the police (in the case of loss or theft) and the Department for Work and Pensions (if a service user's order book is lost or stolen) should also be notified immediately.

Insurance

Providing care in people's homes always carries some risk. It is a registration requirement, under Standard 23 of the National Minimum Standards (see Appendix 1), that the home care provider has adequate insurance for all aspects of their business, 'including the agency's legal liabilities to any and all employees and third party persons to a limit of indemnity commensurate with the level and extent of activities undertaken'. Agencies that use volunteers must also be clear that their insurance covers volunteers as well as employees.

Employer's liability insurance provides cover for any legal liability to any employee of the policy holder resulting from damage to their property, or for injury, illness or disease caused by their employment. Public liability insurance provides cover should the policy holder be legally liable for injury, loss or damage to a third party, or their property, including theft by the employee. Damage to the service user's property should include accidental damage. A registered insurance broker should be able to advise on the cover that is required.

Home care providers should ensure that their procedures do not contravene or invalidate their insurance. They should also check their insurance if any changes are planned to those procedures, and to their service provision.

Self-employed home care workers should have public liability insurance, and service users are advised to check. If service users employ their own home care workers, they should check carefully what their household policy covers in respect of this situation, and what changes or additions they may need to make.

Home care providers, home care workers and service users should be clear about what is covered by: the agency's insurance; the home care worker's insurance; and the service user's insurance (although it should not be assumed that the service user will have insurance). This can minimise difficulties if, for example, the service user's money is stolen from the home care worker in the course of their work – a thief might snatch a bag that contains both the home care worker's own purse and the state pension which has just been collected for the service user. All parties must also be clear about any limitations made by the insurance company (such as limiting cover when carrying money or valuables to specified amounts away from the home, if this is covered – often £250) and these should not be exceeded. If for any reason it does have to be exceeded, there should be a written agreement between the service user and the home care worker (who may not be willing to take responsibility for items of greater value), and it should be clear that the liability lies with the service user. If home care workers know that a service user does not have appropriate insurance, they could help them seek advice about any appropriate and reasonable insurance policies that are available. However, the final decision must always be the service user's.

Emergency protection of service user's property

It is possible that home care workers will find themselves in a situation that requires the service user's immediate admission to hospital or a care home. Most commonly, this will be because of sudden illness or a fall that requires immediate attention. Other situations include fire or flood damage to the service user's home.

There must be clear procedures for the home care worker if they cannot gain access to the house and there are concerns that the service user is at risk. If there is no reply after trying to raise an answer, the police or ambulance service may need to be called. It should be their decision whether it is necessary to break in. A home care worker should never break in to a service user's property without authorisation.

Procedures should cover the protection of property if the service user has to be removed from the house. If the person requires hospital treatment and is conscious, the home care worker should ensure that the person takes with them the items they want from the house. Once the house is securely locked, the service user should be given the key.

If the service user is unconscious or seriously injured or ill, procedures should be in place for the safekeeping of the key. Keys should not just be given to neighbours unless it is known that such a key-holding arrangement with the service user already exists.

Local authority's duty to protect property

Local authorities have a duty under Section 48 of the National Assistance Act 1948, to provide temporary protection of a property if:

- a person has been admitted to hospital or care home;
- a person is unable to look after it themselves;
- it appears there is a danger of loss from or damage to the property.

If the local authority has been involved in the admission of the service user to hospital, it has a clear responsibility to make sure that the property is appropriately safeguarded. Otherwise, the local authority would only become involved if the need to take protective action is brought to its attention. The local authority has a mandatory duty to provide this service if no other suitable arrangements have been made.

The nature of the protection depends on the individual circumstances. It could include ensuring the property is secured (particularly if the premises had been broken into at the time when the service user was taken into hospital), informing the police that the property is empty, taking an inventory and removing items of value to a safe place, ensuring pets are cared for, making arrangements for utilities to be turned off, and disposing of perishable foods.

Local authorities have the power to enter the house and the local authority's procedures should be clear that, in this case, two members of staff should be present when the property is entered and an inventory should be made. The Act also allows the local authority to recoup any reasonable expenses it incurs, from the service user or their spouse.

Case study

Mrs White was taken to hospital following a stroke. The home care worker, Sharon Dailey, who was employed by a voluntary agency, had been unable to get in and the police had forced the door. Mrs White had no relatives in the country – her daughter was in Australia so would be unable to arrive for a few days, even once she was contacted. Mrs White was not friendly with her neighbours. Sharon had rung her supervisor to explain what was happening. She expressed her worries about the amount of money and jewellery she knew Mrs White kept in the house, the fact that there was only going to be a temporary repair to the door and that Mrs White had three cats to be looked after. Mrs White had not previously been known to social services but, because no suitable arrangements could be made, two social workers arrived promptly from the local authority. The police arranged a locksmith to secure the door, and the two social workers undertook an inventory and removed the money and jewellery for safekeeping and arranged for the cats to go into a cattery until the daughter arrived.

KEY POINTS FROM THIS CHAPTER

Do:
- discuss with service users any measures that will help them feel safe;
- find out about local and national home security schemes;
- make sure that there are safe procedures for key-holding and that the service user is aware of them;
- always carry an identity card;
- always knock on the door and get permission to enter first;
- report concerns about rogue traders or bogus callers;
- be aware of safety and security measures that home care workers can take when looking after a service user's money or possessions;
- be aware of any insurance limitations with respect to money and belongings, and do not carry more than the amount specified;
- make sure that the property is safe if the service user's home is suddenly left empty.

Don't:
- frighten older people by overemphasising risks;
- leave keys with neighbours unless there is written permission to do so;
- enter a service user's property without knocking and asking permission;
- leave it to the service user to ask to see your card – always hand it to the service user and do not enter until they have had chance to check it;
- get into a routine when collecting a service user's money or advertise in any way that it is a home care worker collecting it;
- carry more money at any one time than is covered by insurance;
- leave it to a neighbour to sort out the property, unless the service user has agreed to that, should they have to leave suddenly.

7

Gifts, wills and bequests

Many service users are very grateful for the help they receive from their home care workers and want to show their gratitude in the form of gifts, or treats such as taking them out for a meal, or sometimes bequests in their wills. When there is a long-standing relationship between the home care worker and the service user, friendships often develop. This can cause a number of problems, particularly if home care workers have continued to visit, either to work in a private capacity or as a friend, and have been left bequests. This chapter explores the issues concerning gifts and bequests, and Appendix 2 gives summaries of some recent reports from the Local Government Ombudsman that illustrate some of the areas of difficulty.

Custom, practice and procedures

Normally the acceptance of gifts will be governed by the home care worker's contract of employment. It is against established practice for home care workers to accept gifts, and certainly they should never be accepted as an inducement, and never be solicited. In addition, home care workers employed by local authorities will be governed by codes of conduct, issued under Section 82 of the Local Government Act 2000.

The General Social Care Council has issued a code of practice for all social care workers and their employers, which states that 'as a social care worker, you must strive to establish and maintain the trust and confidence of service users and their carers. This includes ... adhering to policies and procedures about accepting gifts and money from service users and carers'.

Under the National Minimum Standards (see Appendix 1), registered home care agencies must have policies and procedures in place covering not accepting gifts and cash (beyond a *very* minimal value).

When a local authority contracts with a home care agency, written agreement should be recorded regarding any gifts/bequests policy to be followed. It is vital that staff and service users are clear about the policy to avoid misunderstandings.

The fact that a home care worker has received and read the policy and procedures on gifts should be recorded in writing and placed on file. This point was specifically picked up in one of the Ombudsman cases (99/B/1651) outlined in Appendix 2, in which the council could not show that a home care worker had received an instruction about gifts. This was regarded as maladministration.

Although volunteers in schemes run by the local authority are not officers of that authority, care needs to be taken that they are aware of the authority's gifts/bequests policy and make a written undertaking to follow it. This should also apply to organisations such as charities that introduce volunteers to service users.

Through training and team meetings, home care workers should have the opportunity to explore some of the issues raised by gifts and bequests from the perspectives of all concerned, including the service user and their relatives. If relatives challenge a gift or bequest, the home care worker needs to be aware that this could lead to all aspects of their work with the service user being scrutinised to establish that no undue influence was exerted. In some cases, the service user's will may be challenged, or a complaint made to the agency or the local authority.

Visiting in a private capacity

Home care workers and service users should be clear that the procedures about gifts and bequests still apply if they undertake any additional, private work for the service user. Many local authorities and agencies have particular policies about undertaking private work for service users, as they are aware of the possible conflicts of interest that can arise. As long as the home care worker continues to be employed by a local authority or an agency, they should be bound by the policy and procedures of that local authority or agency when undertaking private work or visiting any person who they know through their employment.

Policies and procedures in relation to gifts and bequests should also extend to the family of the home care worker.

Accepting gifts

It must be recognised that denying the service user the opportunity of expressing their thanks by buying a gift could undermine the principle of choice in the way the service user spends their money. A compromise can be reached by agreeing that a small gift of a personal nature can be accepted for birthdays and Christmas (or other festivals or celebrations when it is customary to give presents). Standard 13 of the National Minimum Standards (see Appendix 1) makes a specific mention of the requirement to have a policy regarding not accepting gifts or cash (beyond a *very* minimal value). Great care needs to be exercised in the acceptance of gifts and bequests to ensure that home care workers do not, and cannot be seen to, exert undue influence on the service users. Often it is family members who raise complaints about large gifts of money or goods to home care workers.

Home care workers should never solicit gifts in any way and need to take great care that expressions of admiration for an item (such as a vase, a piece of furniture or jewellery) are not construed as hints that it should be given to them. Home care workers should always report any gifts or offers of gifts to their manager, who should record them and also monitor the frequency of such gifts.

It is essential that service users are clear that offering gifts should always be discouraged by the home care worker. Service users should be given details on the policy for gifts and bequests. If small gifts are allowed, service users should be given information about what constitutes a gift that could be accepted within the procedures. One person's idea of a gift of very minimal value might not be another's.

Service users should be made aware that all gifts must be reported to the home care worker's manager. Any guidance given to service users should discourage them from making suggestions that home care workers should just keep gifts and not tell anyone. The clearer the service users are about the policy on gifts, the easier it will be to avoid upset and offence, and minimise the risk of having to refuse or return a gift.

There will be times when a gift may be considered to have greater value than can be accepted. Special consideration should be given if the gift is an item that might have sentimental value to family members of the service user.

Case study

Diane, who has been a home care worker for Mrs Rush for five years, is getting married. Mrs Rush, who loves doing cross-stitch, has made her a beautiful wedding sampler which she has had framed. Diane is worried about accepting it, as she is aware that the cost is high – the silks and frame will have come to about £30. At first, her manager says 'no', as the policy is that no gift should be worth more than £5. Mrs Rush is furious, as she so wanted Diane to have this personal gift. Her daughter contacts the line manager to point out that the gift was made specially for Diane and has no value to anyone else, and how upset her mother is to think that Diane cannot have the pleasure of it. The manager agrees that, on this occasion, the gift can be accepted and writes to acknowledge it, making it clear that this is an exception.

Service users should be made aware that all gifts will be acknowledged in writing from the home care worker's manager. The service user will be aware from this that the gift has been reported. A standard letter could be used, which thanks the service user and reinforces the message that only occasional small gifts are permitted.

Money should never be accepted as a gift, unless it is clear that the service user has no opportunity to arrange for a gift to be bought for the home care worker. In these cases, the home care worker should discuss with the service user what they will buy with the money, and report it to their manager. Any subsequent letter from the manager to the service user should refer to the item that has been bought.

When home care workers are directly employed by the service user, care should be taken to discourage gifts or only accept small gifts. Letters should always be written to acknowledge the gift, making it clear that such gifts, whilst appreciated, are in no way sought.

Borrowing and lending

Home care workers and their families should never borrow from or lend money or goods to service users. It is easy for misunderstandings to arise in such situations. Home care workers should never divulge any of their own money problems to service users, who may worry about them and want to try to help. Under no circumstances should a service user feel pressured into helping out a home care worker who may be facing financial difficulty.

Wills and bequests

Home care workers need to take great care with regard to wills and bequests. Standard 13 of the National Minimum Standards states: 'The agency's policies and practices regarding service user's wills and bequests preclude the involvement of any staff or members of their family, in the making of or benefiting from service user's wills or soliciting any other form of bequest or legacy or acting as witness or executor or being involved in any way with any other legal document.'

Procedures should be in place which make it clear that home care workers and their families should not be party to amending or altering wills, or agree to be an executor or witness the signing of a service user's will. All procedures regarding wills and bequests should be signed as having been read and understood by home care workers.

Home care workers must understand the policy regarding bequests and any consequences that may arise from their acceptance. If the policy is that the home care worker would lose their job if they accept a bequest, then service users should be made aware of this in the information they are given about the service. Clear procedures are needed for situations:

- when the home care worker is told that the service user plans to name them in their will;
- when it is discovered, only after the service user's death, that the home care worker is a beneficiary.

If the procedures link in with conditions of employment or codes of conduct, they should be written in consultation with personnel staff.

Once the procedures are established, consideration should be given to informing all local solicitors so that they are aware of them should service users want to discuss naming a home care worker as a beneficiary.

If a home care worker is made aware that a service user intends to name them or any member of their family as a beneficiary in their will, this should be discouraged and must be reported to their manager. The manager should discuss this with the service user and explain the policy of the agency, especially if the policy is that no bequests can be accepted. The service user should be encouraged to discuss the bequest and the agency's policy in detail with their solicitor before making any decisions. All discussions regarding the proposed bequest should be carefully recorded on the service user's file.

Procedures should be in place so that the home care worker is clear about their responsibility to inform their manager as soon as possible and whether they would be allowed to accept the bequest. If home care workers who are directly employed by the service user become aware that they may be named as a beneficiary, they should also encourage independent discussion with a solicitor.

Sometimes bequests to home care workers only come to light when the will is read, after the service user's death. Great care needs to be taken in writing procedures, therefore, and all staff should be aware of the consequences, if any, of them accepting the bequest. It must be remembered that it should always be the free decision of the service user how they want to leave their money.

KEY POINTS FROM THIS CHAPTER

Do:
- ensure that the policy and procedures on gifts and bequests are signed by all those who visit older people, both staff and volunteers;
- ensure that, whilst the home care worker is employed in a professional or voluntary capacity, the policy of the agency still applies, even if they are visiting privately;
- ensure that service users are aware of the policy on gifts and bequests;
- always acknowledge gifts in writing;
- discourage service users from leaving bequests to home care workers, wherever possible;
- always inform the manager if a bequest has been left, before accepting it.

Don't:
- ever solicit gifts;
- ever be a signatory, witness or executor to a will;
- talk to service users about your own financial problems;
- lend service users money, or borrow from them;
- accept gifts without informing a manager.

8 Responding to financial abuse

This chapter explores issues for home care workers and their managers when dealing with cases of financial abuse, suspected financial abuse or theft. It looks at the current state of knowledge, legislation and guidance on the subject, the dilemmas that can be raised, and practice in relation to financial abuse either by someone within the service user's circle of friends or family, or by those who are acting in an official capacity. Anyone who visits service users in an official capacity – sheltered housing workers, volunteers, home care workers – may, at some stage, have concerns about possible financial abuse.

What is financial abuse?

Financial abuse is an act, or a failure to act, by someone in a position of trust. It can include theft, fraud, exploitation, pressure in connection with wills, property, inheritance or financial transactions, or the misuse or misappropriation of property, possessions or benefits.

Financial abuse can take place at any time, in any place. Anybody can potentially be abused, although people whose mental capacity to make decisions for themselves is reducing may be most at risk. Anybody can potentially be an abuser: relatives and family members, friends, neighbours, professional and care staff, home care workers or volunteers, or other service users.

Home care workers are in a good position to spot the first signs that service users are being abused, and are often their main point of contact to get help. One of the problems, however, is that much financial abuse is *hidden* abuse. The way service users have developed their financial dealings may expose them to potential abuse. Some service users will seem to accept actions such as pooling their benefits into the household pot with their family carers, or allowing their spouse or partner to have complete control over the couple's finances. This could be because they think this is the norm, or they fear making a stand, or are quite happy with the arrangement. Other actions by service users, such as handing over their purse or loose change to a local shopkeeper, can also be open to abuse.

Other examples of hidden financial abuse can include:

- the belief instilled in service users by their offspring or other relatives that the service user's possessions are, or will eventually be, theirs, which can influence the way service users spend their money, or arrange their lives;
- lack of willingness to take the time to teach (or re-teach) money-handling skills to a service user, who may be recovering from a stroke, for example;
- imposing other people's financial priorities on the service user;
- making assumptions about the service user's ability to cope with their finances and so withholding financial information.

There are also more overt or conscious actions by those in a position of trust, which deprive service users of their possessions such as taking money or goods without permission, applying duress to hand over control of money or property, or withholding money for necessities, so leaving the person without.

Other forms of abuse

Abuse is defined by the charity Action on Elder Abuse as: 'A single or repeated act or lack of appropriate action occurring within any relationship where there is an expectation of trust which causes harm or distress to an older person'.

Financial abuse is just one aspect of abuse. It is not unknown for other forms of abuse to occur alongside financial abuse. These other forms of abuse have been listed in the guidance, *No Secrets* (Department of Health), as:

- physical abuse, including hitting, slapping, pushing, kicking, misuse of medication, restraint or inappropriate sanctions;
- sexual abuse, including rape and sexual assault or sexual acts to which the vulnerable adult has not consented, or could not consent or was pressured into consenting;
- psychological abuse, including emotional abuse, threats of harm or abandonment, deprivation of contact, humiliation, blaming, controlling, intimidation, coercion, harassment, verbal abuse, isolation or withdrawal from services or supportive networks;
- neglect and acts of omission, including ignoring medical or physical care needs, failure to provide access to appropriate health, social care or educational services, the withholding of the necessities of life such as medication, adequate nutrition and heating;
- discriminatory abuse, including racist, sexist, that based on a person's disability, and other forms of harassment, slurs or similar treatment.

Discriminatory abuse can also be related to a person's age or sexual orientation.

It is possible that the service user could suffer from one or more types of abuse. For example, if relatives are withholding the service user's money, there may also be neglect in that the service user does not get the appropriate amount of food or essential goods, and psychological abuse as the service user's feelings of self-worth may be significantly affected.

The home care worker's role and financial abuse

Many of the good practice guidelines highlighted throughout this book should help minimise and prevent financial abuse, either deliberate, hidden or unintentional. These should be backed up with clear, professional standards and procedures that are both implemented and monitored. Standard 14 of the National Minimum Standards covers the protection of the service user (see Appendix 1).

Home care workers need to think carefully about their actions, and whether, however unintentionally, they might actually be abusive. This could include not maintaining strict confidentiality, not explaining the change from shopping, or not taking care of someone's possessions, which might not be of any monetary value but have a great sentimental value to the service user. When a home care worker sees a colleague not following procedures on the handling of finances and risking abuse of the service user, however unintentionally, concerns should be reported to the manager. The General Social Care Council's code of practice on protecting service users states that this 'includes informing the employer or an appropriate authority where the practice of colleagues may be unsafe or adversely affecting standards of care'. This enables the manager to take appropriate action or use opportunities in supervision sessions to stress the importance of following procedures. Actual theft by colleagues should always be reported immediately.

Case study

Mr Green's finances had become the responsibility of social services and a package of care, using a home care worker from a private agency, had been set up. The social worker responsible for managing his finances was on long-term sick leave and her work was taken on by her line manager. Mr Green's son became concerned and reported to the social services that there was little evidence of the shopping that was supposed to have been done, that the food bought was inappropriate, and that receipts which were provided included costs for items that were never apparent in Mr Green's home. Eventually, a complaint was made to the Local Government Ombudsman. The council agreed that there was inadequate monitoring of the care plan and of the financial arrangements. Withdrawals of Mr Green's money from the office safe were not always recorded, and there was a considerable amount of money that could not be accounted for. The home care worker had left the agency and could not be traced. As a result of the complaint, the council paid £5,460 to reimburse the money that could not be accounted for, and a further £2,000 in compensation. The Ombudsman found maladministration and called for the council to ensure there was no repetition of such failures to monitor. (Local Government Ombudsman report 00/C/10708, 21 June 2001)

Further efforts in preventing abuse are needed, to ensure that anyone visiting older people in their own homes understands and is aware of the different forms of abuse, can recognise the early signs and knows the procedures to follow on suspected abuse. Home care workers should always encourage service users to seek help, if they think they are being abused. Training should be provided to all staff and volunteers who visit service users.

ⓘ Further information and confidential advice on tackling abuse can be obtained from one of the national help lines, including Action on Elder Abuse, Counsel and Care, and Public Concern at Work (see Appendix 4 for contact details).

Indications of financial abuse

Home care workers need to be careful not to make assumptions about the risk of abuse or jump to hasty conclusions. However, there are signs that might raise suspicions of possible financial abuse, including:

- unexplained withdrawals from the service user's savings account;
- unpaid bills;
- sudden shortages of money in spite of an adequate income;
- difficulties in accessing adequate funds for the service user's day-to-day needs when family or friends have control of the money;
- the disappearance of money or valuables from the house;
- the sudden transfer of assets to a relative;
- changes in the behaviour of the service user;
- the service user's inability to explain what is happening to their money.

Whilst research into abuse in general, including financial abuse, has been limited, there are certain situations that have been identified as being associated with abuse, including:

- the financial dependency of the informal or family carer on the service user (or vice versa);
- when service users have a disability that affects their memory and ability to reason;

- when the carer or family experience an unfavourable change in their financial circumstances, or require money to maintain an expensive lifestyle;
- when the carer has had to change their lifestyle as a result of caring.

Home care workers should be alert to these situations. However, it should be noted that, as with all aspects of abuse, there is still a great deal to be learned in both recognising the situations and then dealing with them.

Legislation and guidance

There is no single or specific piece of legislation that deals with abuse (including financial abuse). However, most forms of abuse are illegal: for example, financial abuse is theft. When the service user is unable to make an informed decision, or understand the implications of a particular decision, there can be very limited power to intervene. The Court of Protection or the Department for Work and Pensions can revoke the powers of a registered attorney, receiver or appointee, who acts on behalf of a person who lacks mental capacity (see Chapter 5), if any of these people are using their position of trust to financially abuse the service user. Also, in cases of the receiver being the abuser, there is a security bond and the insurance company should make good the loss. It may then take steps to recover funds from the person who has taken the money.

Service users themselves can prosecute under the Theft Act 1968 or, if it is not possible to prove financial abuse 'beyond reasonable doubt', which is the test required by criminal law, but merely 'on the balance of probabilities', they can pursue a civil remedy. If service users are considering any legal remedy, they should be advised to seek independent legal advice.

Guidance in England on handling abuse has been issued (*No Secrets*, Department of Health) for multi-agency collaboration and developing local policies and procedures. There is similar guidance in Wales (*In Safe Hands*). Social services departments have been given the lead role in co-ordinating any policy guidance, and there must be multi-agency procedures in place locally. These local procedures should help home care workers and their managers to ensure that they are taking the appropriate action. They should include:

- the various roles and responsibilities of different staff and organisations;
- a statement of the procedures for dealing with allegations of abuse;
- a statement about what to do in the event of failure to take the necessary action;
- a full list of points of referral, indicating how to access support, advice and protection at all times (including outside normal working hours);
- an indication of how to record allegations of abuse;
- a list of expert sources of advice;
- the inter-agency procedures for decision making;
- a list of all services that might offer victims access to support or redress.

All registered home care providers must have procedures on financial abuse as a distinct part of their procedures on abuse in general. These are required as part of Standard 14 of the National Minimum Standards (see Appendix 1). Guidance should also be included in any procedures on handling service user's finances. All home care workers must have copies of the procedures and should be aware whether this guidance forms part of an agreed procedure by all agencies in the area.

It must be recognised that home care workers are in the front line and amongst those most likely to identify cases of abuse. The procedures should give home care workers a clear framework that supports them in their judgements about what actions to take to protect service users who are suffering financial abuse. All home care workers should have the opportunity, through training and supervision, to explore their own views about financial abuse and their role within the procedures.

Dealing with financial abuse

Service user's choice and confidentiality

Home care workers and their managers should recognise the potential conflict between the service user's right to choose (which could include remaining in a position where there is financial abuse) and their concerns about protecting the service user. If the service user decides to remain in a position of financial abuse, measures should be taken to protect them, as far as possible. Some service users will want to protect the abuser, especially if it is a relative, and might decide that the relationship with the abuser is more important than stopping the abuse. Others might fear what the abuser will do if they are accused, or feel that no one would believe them or be able to help them. Service users who lack mental capacity may not be in a position to recognise that financial abuse is happening to them. If the service user has fluctuating mental capacity, it may be necessary to investigate whether arrangements should be made to help the person with their finances (see Chapter 5).

When the service user decides to remains in an abusive situation, there should be regular monitoring and review, and the home care worker should report regularly to their manager. Written records should be kept on the actions or decisions taken.

It is vital that all service users are aware from the outset of the situations that home care workers must report to their manager and ask for guidance on how to proceed. Self-employed or directly-employed home care workers may need to contact one of the national help lines, such as Action on Elder Abuse or Counsel and Care (see Appendix 4 for contact details) for advice and guidance on tackling abuse. Home care workers should never discuss their concerns with, or challenge, a possible abuser. This could alert the person and perhaps make an investigation more difficult, and even put the service user at risk.

Home care workers should be clear when there is a duty to take action and never promise a degree of confidentiality they cannot keep. Information should only be shared, on a 'need to know' basis, when it is in the best interests of the service user. Initial decisions will usually be taken by the manager as to whether the case is referred on, and to whom it is referred, following local procedures and guidance issued in *No Secrets* (Department of Health). Any planned action should be discussed with the service user beforehand. Their wishes should always be respected unless other people could be at risk.

Case study

Mr Johnson had been receiving home care services twice a week since his wife died six years ago. Recently, his elder daughter and her husband had moved back to live with her father following the collapse of their business. Mr Johnson expected this to be short term, and his home care services continued.

Over time, his home care worker, Mrs Scholl, noticed changes. He had begun to spend less time in his lounge, and was often found sitting alone in his bedroom when she called in the afternoon. She reported her concerns to her manager, although Mr Johnson assured her that he was quite happy. He said the same thing to his care manager, who visited following Mrs Scholl's report.

The daughter then said that she would do the shopping and collect Mr Johnson's pension, and so Mrs Scholl only needed to visit once a week. Mr Johnson agreed to this but Mrs Scholl was worried. She had known him for a long time and, over the next few weeks, she gently questioned him about what food he was getting. Eventually, Mr Johnson confided that his daughter had taken complete control of his money. She had moved his savings into a joint account and had persuaded him to transfer the house into her name. He seemed very relieved to be telling someone what was happening, but became agitated when Mrs Scholl began to outline what steps she could take in response. He could not take action against his daughter and refused to allow her to do anything; he just wanted to talk to her about it.

Mrs Scholl explained that she would have to report back to her office but that no action would be taken without his agreement. After a case conference, the care manager visited, but Mr Johnson insisted he wanted no action taken. Instead, a strategy was adopted of monitoring and encouraging, and ensuring that his daughter was aware that the care manager was keeping an eye on things. Mrs Scholl had regular meetings with her own manager and the care manager to support her in the current situation of knowing that the daughter was financially abusing her father. Before Mr Johnson eventually died, he had become 'bedroom-bound', unable to purchase clothing or personal items without his daughter's involvement and he had lost much of his quality of life. He maintained right to the end, however, that the relationship with his daughter was more important than anything else. The weekly visits from his home care worker, who he knew understood the position, had been a great help to him.

Keeping records

Within the procedures on abuse, there should be clear guidelines on reporting concerns about financial abuse. A written record should be made as soon as possible after discovery. Great care needs to be taken about what is recorded in a service user's visit record that is kept at home, especially if the person suspected of financially abusing the service user might have access to that record. More detailed records should be made in a special record/file kept for the purpose and on the service user's case file held in the office. Once the home care worker has recorded the concerns they have about possible financial abuse, and discussed the situation with their line manager, decisions will need to be made according to the multi-agency guidelines on the action to be taken. It is essential that the situation is kept under review and case notes kept up-to-date, especially if no action has been taken to remove the person from the abuser. Evidence of abuse may be required in cases where action is taken.

Deciding what action will be taken

Deciding what action will be taken is normally a team decision and will include consideration of:

- an investigation, within a jointly agreed framework, to determine the facts of the case;
- the extent of the risk;
- what actions can minimise the risk;

- who takes that action;
- who should monitor the action;
- reviewing the plan.

Supporting the home care worker

Home care workers should be supported, through supervision and training, when they are helping the service user through any investigation of financial abuse and dealing with the after-effects. Support may also be necessary to help home care workers understand and accept situations in which the service user is aware of possible abuse but does not wish to take the matter further. It is important that anyone visiting a service user in a voluntary or professional capacity is confident that, if they have concerns about possible or actual financial abuse, there is someone to whom they can report this and that the matter will be dealt with promptly.

Although it is likely to be other professionals (care managers and senior staff and sometimes the police) who are involved in the investigation, the home care worker is probably the most frequent visitor and will need to respond to the service user's feelings about the situation. Even though the service user might have agreed to action being taken, they could start to feel that things are now out of their control, or worried about what will happen to the abuser, and to themselves. They could be angry at, or even abusive to, the home care worker, if they were the person who first recognised that financial abuse had occurred. Home care workers should be supported in handling these sometimes extremes of emotion, both through ongoing training sessions and more regular supervision when dealing with specific cases. Home care workers should know who is handling the case and who they can contact for further information or advice.

If the service user decides not to take any action and remains in a situation where financial abuse is continuing, options should be explored to help the service user to minimise any further abuse. Although the wishes of service users must be respected, home care workers should be alert to any possibility of them changing their minds. Some victims of abuse need time before they feel able or empowered to take action.

Responding to financial abuse by staff

There will be times when home care workers or volunteers are themselves involved in, or suspected of, financial abuse. This could be discovered in the following ways:

- the line manager picks up inconsistencies during routine monitoring of receipts;
- another care worker suspects or finds out that a colleague (either within the same agency or from another provider) has been financially abusing a service user;
- the service user or their family make an allegation that the home care worker has taken money, or exerted influence on the service user to make them a gift or bequest.

It is essential that all providers take any concerns about their home care workers very seriously and have procedures in place to investigate and deal with the situation. Investigations should be co-ordinated if there is more than one agency involved. As a matter of course, allegations of criminal behaviour should be reported to the police. The standard of proof for prosecution is 'beyond reasonable doubt'. The standard of proof for internal disciplinary procedures is 'on the balance of probabilities'.

Home care workers should be aware of the organisation's policy on dealing with abuse that is suspected or carried out by staff. It should be made clear, during training and supervision, the procedures that would have to be followed if there was ever an allegation of abuse against the home care worker. This should help them understand what would happen, in advance of any problems, especially in situations when they are subject to the rigours of an investigation but the allegation is proved to be unfounded.

Home care workers who have been accused of financial abuse should be clearly advised of their rights under employment legislation, the internal disciplinary procedures and where they can seek advice or support. They should also be informed of their right to representation and, if necessary, where to find a representative.

Case study

Tony and Derek had lived in a long-stay hostel for people with learning disabilities for many years. They were assessed as being able to live together in the community with support from a social worker and the home care service, and they were allocated a council flat. John was assigned as their home care worker. He had been employed for about two years and was highly respected by his other clients. Although John had his personal problems, which he had discussed with his supervisor, they were such that his work was not affected in any way.

One of John's tasks was to supervise Tony and Derek's income and expenditure. John was responsible for their budgeting and ensuring any surplus income was banked appropriately. Financial recording systems were set up in the home and John completed the details on a daily basis. John's supervisor was required to check the financial records at regular intervals. Tony and Derek's circumstances were regularly reviewed by the social worker.

Over a period of time, the social worker noticed that the amount deposited for savings had drastically reduced and instigated an investigation. It was revealed that the home care supervisor had not been checking the financial records thoroughly and that John had been taking a substantial amount each week from Tony and Derek's income. It was also revealed that John had a gambling addiction that had not been discussed previously with his supervisor, and he had been using the money to support this habit. The amount involved was difficult to calculate but was thought to be in the region of £5,000.

The police were informed and John was charged with theft. He pleaded guilty and was sentenced to six months imprisonment. The supervisor was disciplined and received a final written warning for not following financial procedures.

Home care workers may be suspended, pending the outcome of the investigation. Arrangements should be made for them to receive support during this time, and every effort should be made to ensure that they are given as much information as can be allowed within the investigation. It should be remembered that not all allegations are true. Decisions not to suspend should be fully documented and endorsed by a senior member of the service provider. Sometimes genuine mistakes can be made, when the home care worker is accused of financial abuse but the money is later found to have been mislaid, hidden or given to someone else, which the service user has forgotten. If the complaint proves to be unfounded, home care workers should be advised of how they can seek redress. They should also receive support to help ease them back into work, cope with their feelings, and be offered counselling, if necessary.

Sometimes home care workers might be afraid of 'blowing the whistle' on a colleague. Under the Public Interest Disclosure Act 1998, home care workers can seek support from Public Concern at Work (see Appendix 4) or their trade union, which aim to protect workers who speak out 'in good faith'. Any agency or local authority has a duty of care towards users of its services and, if a colleague has been financially abusing a service user, that duty of care has been broken. The General Social Care Council, set up in April 2002, will hold a register which will cover all staff and employers in the care professions, including home care workers. People found to be unsuitable to work with vulnerable adults can be struck off this register.

i Action on Elder Abuse provides a range of information leaflets and papers on elder abuse, including: *The abuse of older people at home; Speaking out on elder abuse; Bags of money;* and *The great taboo.* See Appendix 4 for contact details.

KEY POINTS FROM THIS CHAPTER

Do:

- develop good practices to avoid any unintentional financial abuse;
- follow procedures that have been developed to help eliminate financial abuse;
- be aware of the indications of financial abuse;
- be aware of the specific procedures in place regarding financial abuse;
- report any concerns about financial abuse to a manager;
- keep good records;
- help support the service user through the investigations and the outcome;
- be aware of organisations that offer information and advice on abuse.

Don't:

- ignore indications of financial abuse;
- confront the person doing the financial abusing;
- promise confidentiality when it cannot be kept;
- be afraid to report a colleague if financial abuse is suspected.

9 Collecting charges

This chapter explores the involvement of home care workers (employed by local authorities or independent home care agencies) in collecting charges from service users. It also explores the issues concerning billing arrangements and non-payment of bills. The second part of the chapter specifically relates to the charging policies of local authorities, and outlines the legislation and Department of Health (DH) guidance that govern those policies. It looks finally at the involvement of home care providers and their staff in collecting those charges on behalf of the local authority.

Charges for services provided

Whilst most NHS services are free at the point of use, there are very few services providing care and practical help at home that are free, other than volunteer befriending schemes. Local authorities have discretion whether or not to charge for the services they provide to support people in their homes, and only a very small minority do not charge. Even in these areas, other services such as meals-on-wheels or day care may well attract a charge. Service users who arrange their care privately, either through an independent agency or by directly employing a home care worker, will have to pay the agreed price.

Home care workers involvement with charges

Home care workers should have as little involvement as possible in the collection of the charges, and never just for the administrative convenience of the organisation. It involves them in financial transactions, even if it has been agreed they should not be involved in any other aspects of the service user's finances. There are also issues of confidentiality if home care workers collect charges that have been assessed by the local authority, as the way the charge has been calculated could mean that the home care worker will have some knowledge of that service user's finances. If there is no alternative, any arrangements should be governed by the organisation's procedures. A home care worker's involvement with collecting charges should normally only include those transactions that are undertaken at a post office, or posting a cheque in the same way as the home care worker undertakes other financial transactions (see Chapter 2). Procedures should cover issues such as the proper receipting and security arrangements for staff when handing over the charges to the provider. They should also cover what to do if the service user does not pay.

Home care workers should never have to rely on the service user paying a charge to make up their own wages, unless they are directly employed by the service user. To be so reliant could create a conflict of interest between the home care worker and the service user, especially if circumstances change and the service user is unable to pay the money.

Billing arrangements

Service providers should give their service users clear, written information on how much they will be expected to pay for the services they receive. This should include:

- what is included in the price;
- the methods by which it can be paid;
- whether there would be extra charges for services not included in the care package or contract agreed with the provider;
- whether the service user will be charged if they fail to notify the provider of their absence;
- how the price will be affected if the provider fails to provide the agreed service;
- how frequently prices will be reviewed;
- the period of notice for changes to the price;
- who to contact if they have any queries about the costs.

Service users should be offered as much choice as possible in how they pay for the costs of their care. They should also be provided with information from the service provider on the various methods of payment available, and whether any would incur extra handling costs to the service user. The method of payment chosen by the service user should be recorded on file and the appropriate procedures put in place.

Non-payment of bills

Service users should be made aware of their responsibility to pay bills promptly from the outset and of any consequences of non-payment of charges. Any non-payment, either for services directly purchased from an independent home care provider or of local authority charges, should be recorded on file and followed up promptly. Home care workers, who collect money for the charges on behalf of the service provider, should be aware of the procedures to be followed in the event of non-payment.

When the service provider follows up non-payment, great care should be exercised in establishing the reasons. It may be because the service user:

- does not understand what they have to pay;
- is becoming forgetful;
- cannot afford the cost of the service, which may indicate the need for benefits advice or, in the case of a service arranged by a local authority, a reduction in the charge;
- has family members or friends who have neglected to pay on the service user's behalf;
- has taken a political or personal decision not to pay the service provider's charge.

When the service user has directly-bought services from an agency or self-employed care worker, it may be part of the contract that non-payment can lead to service withdrawal. Before such action is taken, strenuous efforts should be made to try to resolve the situation. If it is considered that the person would be at some risk if the service were withdrawn, the service user should be encouraged to seek an assessment of their needs from the local authority.

The Department of Health guidance to local authorities makes it clear that, if the service user has not paid the local authority charges, the service cannot be withdrawn because of non-payment. Local authorities can pursue the debt through the civil courts.

Local authorities should have procedures to establish the respective roles of the home care provider in their day-to-day contact with the service user, the manager supervising the care of the service user and of the finance or administrative staff in managing any debt recovery process. Any detailed procedures must be agreed with all parties involved and follow the principle that the service user's welfare is the primary responsibility of the social services department. No action should be taken without the agreement of care management staff.

Local authority charges for care at home

It is important that home care workers and those service users who are charged by local authorities are aware of the legislation, national guidance and the individual policy of the local authority in establishing those charges.

The amount charged for services provided at home varies from as little as £2 or £3 to as much as several hundred pounds a week, as local authorities vary in their interpretation of what is 'reasonable', as laid down in section 17 of the Health and Social Services and Social Security Adjudications Act 1983. In some areas, the service user pays the full cost, if they can afford it. In others, there is a maximum charge that reflects a proportion of the cost of providing the service. Many local authorities have banded charges, based on the income of the service user and the number of hours provided.

The introduction of the Department of Health guidance, from April 2003, should balance out some of these wide variations, but it is still at the discretion of local authorities whether they charge at all, or have a more generous charging policy than that suggested in the guidance.

Legislation and guidance

Local authorities currently charge for services provided at home under Section 17 of the Health and Social Services and Social Security Adjudications (HASSASSA) Act 1983, although charges have been possible since 1948. It is at the discretion of each local authority whether to charge for services other than care in a care home, for which there are national rules.

If a local authority does decide to charge for home care, it has to be 'reasonable', as laid down in section 17 of the HASSASSA Act, and, from April 2003, has to comply with 'tests of reasonableness' in the Department of Health guidance (see page 127). The authority can decide what it considers to be 'reasonable' but, if a service user (or a carer who is receiving carers' services under the Carers and Disabled Children Act 2000) can show the authority that it is not reasonable for them to pay that charge, the local authority should reduce or waive the charge.

DEPARTMENT OF HEALTH GUIDANCE

In November 2001, the Department of Health (DH) issued guidance, *Fairer Charging Policies for Home Care and Other Non-residential Social Services*, which gives a framework within which local authorities set their charges (although there is nothing to stop them from having more generous policies). It includes the following points:

- Local authorities cannot charge for services provided under section 117 of the Mental Health Act 1984 (these are aftercare services for people who have been detained in hospital for treatment for their mental health condition); for anyone receiving Intermediate Care (which is short-term care, normally of less than six weeks to avoid hospital admission or following a stay in hospital); or for anyone who has Creuzfeldt Jacob Disease (CJD).
- Charges should not be levied for any one service in isolation; the impact of charging for one service should be taken into account when assessing the ability to pay for another service.
- All local authorities should consider whether and how to set an overriding 'maximum' charge and should consult service users specifically on this.

- All local authorities should ensure that appropriate benefits advice is provided to all service users and carers at the time of the charging assessment, which should include advice about entitlement, help with completing claim forms and follow-up action, if the service user wishes.
- Only the service user can be charged and their resources looked at in any means test, unless, in individual cases, resources to which the service user has a legal entitlement are held in another's name.
- Information about charges and how they are assessed should be readily available to service users and their carers. Charges should not normally be made for any period before an assessment of charges has been communicated to the service user.
- Service users and carers should be consulted if there are changes to the charging system.
- Service users should know how to ask for a review if it is difficult for them to pay the charge, and know about the local authority complaints procedure.
- Once someone has been assessed as needing a service, that service should not be withdrawn even if the service user refuses to pay. The debt may be pursued through the courts.

In addition, the Department of Health guidance makes the following stipulations about the way income, savings and benefits are to be assessed:

Income and savings

Each authority has its own policy about how it assesses service users' income and savings. However, the Department of Health guidance has made clear that local authorities must not leave service users with an income of less than their defined level of Income Support/MIG (but not necessarily including the Severe Disability Premium) plus a buffer of 25 per cent above that level after paying the charges (see Chapter 4 for an explanation of benefits). The Department of Health guidance has also stated that local authorities should disregard all earnings from any charging assessment.

Local authorities should use the capital limits used in charging for care in a care home as a minimum, and not charge the full cost of the service if the person has less than the upper capital limit (£19,500 in 2003/2004). They can set higher capital limits if they wish.

Disability benefits and disability-related costs

Many authorities charge against a service user's Attendance Allowance (AA) or Disability Living Allowance (Care) (DLA Care), and the Severe Disability Premium (SDP) paid within Income Support/MIG. They often increase the basic charge by a set amount if the service user receives any of these benefits. By law, local authorities cannot charge against the person's mobility component of DLA. It has also been established through the courts that, if a local authority is only providing services during the day (and helping someone get up or go to bed counts as a day service), it cannot charge against any AA/DLA that is paid for night time.

If the local authority charges against AA/DLA or SDP, it must take into account the service user's disability-related costs. The Department of Health guidance lists some of the normal costs such as: additional laundry and dietary costs; extra wear and tear on clothing; heating; gardening or cleaning; equipment; transport.

IMPLEMENTATION OF THE DEPARTMENT OF HEALTH GUIDANCE

Originally, it had been hoped that the Department of Health guidance would have been implemented by local authorities by April 2002. It has now been delayed until 1 April 2003. However, some aspects had to be implemented by 1 October 2002, at the latest:

- Service users receiving Income Support/MIG, whose overall income equals the defined levels plus a buffer of 25 per cent (see page 127), should stop being charged from that date at the latest.
- Service users receiving more than 10 hours a week home care, whose charges take account of their disability benefits (see above), should have an individual assessment of their disability-related expenditure from no later than that date.
- Earnings should be disregarded as part of income from no later than that date.

SUPPORTING PEOPLE SERVICES

From April 2003, people who live in supported or sheltered housing will no longer receive help through their Housing Benefit or Income Support/MIG for the costs of the warden's services and other support services (see Chapter 4). These costs will come under 'Supporting People Services' and there will, in most cases, be a separate charge for them. If a service user receives both Supporting People Services and other care services arranged by the local authority, they will be charged only once for both services, using the local means test for charging for home care services. It will bring many more people into the means test used by the local authority for charging, although there will be protection to ease the change of moving over from national Housing Benefit rules to local rules for charging. People receiving Housing Benefit will not be charged for their Supporting People Services.

Collection of local authority charges

As with the collection of any charges, service users should be given a choice of collection method, and home care workers should have their involvement kept to a minimum.

If the local authority uses independent providers to provide social services' clients with home care under contract, the question arises about who collects the local authority charges.

Local authorities set and recover charges for services arranged by them. However, other agencies can collect the money on their behalf. Local authorities, service providers and service users should be clear that any charges for the service provided under contract to the local authority remain the responsibility of the local authority. If the service provider collects on the local authority's behalf, any non-payment is for the local authority to resolve, and is not the responsibility of the provider. The provider should also not lose out financially if any service user does not pay the charges.

Home care workers and local authority charges

Home care workers will not normally be involved in the local authority's assessment of the service user's finances for charging purposes. In most cases, this will be done by the financial assessors who will help complete the assessment form, and give benefits advice. When the local authority takes disability benefits into account, the person undertaking the assessment should also take into account any extra costs the service user has because of their disability. (See page 126 for the Department of Health guidance that local authorities must follow by April 2003 by the latest.)

Some service users will have no concerns about their charges, and be quite happy to pay them. Others may find them difficult to meet. Home care workers need to be aware of how the local authority has set up any complaints or appeals process and how service users can make representations if they feel their charges are too high.

The more the home care worker knows about the local charging policy, the better they will be able to inform the service user of the points which might be useful to stress in any representations. The home care worker will often have a good knowledge of the extra costs incurred by service users with a disability due to factors such as diet, heating, transport, gardening or domestic cleaning, if this is not part of the home care package.

Home care workers may be the first to pick up on service users who have difficulty meeting the charges. They should be aware when the charging policy changes, as this can sometimes have an effect on service users. The local authority should consult on changes to charging policies, and send information to service users. Sometimes a service user might find the information difficult to understand, or they may want to take part in the consultation but be unable to get to meetings. Home care providers and local authorities, as well as individual home care workers, should consider ways of involving service users in the consultation process.

If a service user wants to withdraw from their service because of the charges, the home care worker should inform their manager as soon as possible. Before any service user withdraws, however, they should be encouraged to seek a review of their charges to see if they can be waived or reduced. They should also seek a reassessment of their needs to ensure that, by withdrawing or lowering the level of service, they are not left at risk.

Case study

Mrs Winfield told her home care worker, Ann, that she did not want her to call any more. Ann knew that the local authority had just changed its charging policy and had been worried how this would affect Mrs Winfield, who had grumbled about the charges several times last year. Ann had suggested then that she should ask for a review but Mrs Winfield had not wanted this. She was very private about her money and so Ann was not sure what money she had coming in. However, she knew from discussions and from working with her that Mrs Winfield had a number of extra costs. These included wear and tear on clothes and increased laundry requirements due to incontinence, large heating bills due to an antiquated heating system, which she had to have on for most of the year because she felt the cold, and taxi fares to visit her daughter who was disabled and living in a care home.

Ann suggested to Mrs Winfield that, before she dropped the service, she should write to the local authority explaining these extra costs and ask for the charges to be reviewed. Mrs Winfield did this and, as a result, her charges were reduced so that they were lower than they had been the previous year!

NB. From April 2003, at the latest, these extra costs should be considered in the assessment of the charge if the local authority is taking account of disability benefits in its assessment (see page 128). Home care workers may still be able to help service users recognise when these costs are 'extras', as service users may have accepted them as 'usual', if they have been paying for them for many years.

Service user's choice in paying the provider

Service users should be given a choice about whether they wish to pay their charge directly to the local authority, or pay the service provider. Particular recognition should be given to the issue of confidentiality, when it is proposed that a provider collects the charge. The service user may not wish the home care agency to be aware of their financial affairs. Many charging policies are structured so the agency would be aware of the type of benefit the service user receives or the amount of capital, if it collected the charges direct.

Should the service user accept that the provider be paid the charge direct, the local authority should ensure through its contracting mechanism that the service user is offered a range of methods of payment, receives prompt, clear statements of their charge and reasons for any variation. In particular, there should be adequate security and receipting arrangements if the service user opts to pay cash.

If the service user also contracts with that provider for other services, they should have a clear account about what is the social services charge and what is the charge for what they are buying directly from the agency. Service users must be given information about their social services charges separately from information about any charge for other services.

KEY POINTS FROM THIS CHAPTER

Do:

- get to know the local authority charging system;
- encourage service users to ask for a reduction if they think the charge is too high;
- try to help the service user choose a payment method that does not involve the home care worker in collection;
- ensure service users are clear about how much they are being charged and reasons for variations, and how to complain;
- ensure service users are offered a choice in the way they pay their charge;
- help service users become involved in any consultation about charges.

Don't:

- let the service user withdraw from the service because of the charges without exploring other ways of helping and seeking a re-assessment of their needs;
- allow home care workers to have to rely on service users paying their charge to make up their wages (unless the service user employs the home care worker direct).

Glossary

Care Manager A person who carries out the major tasks of care management such as assessment, preparing a care plan, co-ordinating services, and monitoring and review. The care manager may control the budget, but is not generally involved in providing a particular care service.

Care Plan A written statement agreed by all parties, setting out the service user's care needs, and the support required to meet those needs. It should be regularly updated.

Commission for Social Care Inspection It will replace the National Care Standards Commission during 2004. This new body will inspect all social care organisations and produce reports of those inspections, inspect local authority social services departments, publish star ratings for social services departments and recommend special measures, when necessary, and publish annual reports to parliament on progress on social care and analysis of the use of resources.

Community Care Services and support to help anyone with care needs to live as independently as possible in their home, wherever that is.

Complaints procedures (independent providers) Under the requirements of the National Minimum Standards, all registered home care providers must provide easily understood, well publicised and accessible procedures to enable service users, their relatives or representative to make a complaint. There are time scales and service users are kept informed at all stages of the investigation of the complaint. If the complaint is not resolved, the service user can complain to the National Care Standards Commission at any stage, if they so wish.

Complaints procedures (local authorities) Social services' statutory complaints procedures have three stages – local resolution (informal), formal, and an independently chaired panel. There are time limits. If the complaint is not resolved, the service user can complain to the Local Government Ombudsman. When social services arrange for care to be provided by an independent organisation (such as a home care agency or a care home) under a contract, the person receiving care is still entitled to use the social services' complaints procedure.

Contracting The process through which local authorities purchase services from private or voluntary organisations.

Department for Work and Pensions (DWP) Formerly the Department of Social Security (DSS).

Domiciliary Care See Home Care.

Domiciliary Care National Minimum Standards These standards, referred to throughout this book as the National Minimum Standards, are a registration requirement for agencies providing personal care in people's own homes. They form the criteria by which the National Care Standards Commission (NCSC) determines whether the agency provides personal care to the required standard. Their purpose is to ensure the quality of personal care and support which people receive whilst living in their own home in the community.

General Social Care Council (GSCC) Sets codes of conduct and practice for staff and employers in care professions, and will hold a general register of those staff. It also regulates social work education and training.

Home Care Personal care and practical services which are provided to support service users to remain in their own homes. It is also known as 'domiciliary care', which is the term used in the National Minimum Standards, although 'home care' is the term mainly used throughout the book.

Home Care Worker Anyone who visits people in their own homes in a professional or voluntary capacity to offer care or practical services. This includes self-employed or directly-employed home care workers, as well as staff and volunteers in a local authority, or a voluntary or independent agency. It also covers housing and health staff who visit people in their own homes.

Home Care Manager The member of staff managing home care workers.

Home Care Provider The organisation providing home care, either an independent agency or a local authority.

Local Government Ombudsman Service A service which can investigate complaints of injustice arising from maladministration in any department of the local authority. It can normally investigate complaints only after the local authority has already had the opportunity to deal with the complaint (usually through the local authority complaints procedure).

National Care Standards Commission (NCSC) The regulatory body that registers care homes and home care agencies which have to meet the National Minimum Standards. It oversees that these standards, relating to the care of service users, are met by agencies providing personal care. It also investigates any complaints against any services that are registered. It will be replaced by the Commission for Social Care Inspection by 2004.

National Minimum Standards See Domiciliary Care National Minimum Standards.

Pensions and Benefits A generic term to cover all state benefits.

Personal Assistant An alternative name for a home care worker, often used for those who are either self-employed or employed directly by the person needing care or support at home, many of whom receive money from the Independent Living Fund or Direct Payments to employ their own worker.

Policies The statements of intent to help staff take decisions which are legal and consistent with the aims of the service, and in the best interests of service users.

Procedures Written guidance for staff on various aspects of their caring tasks, with particular reference to those on handling finances.

They outline the steps taken to fulfil the policies. They may be loose sheets or in a manual.

Registered Person In the Domiciliary Care Agencies Regulations 2002, a registered person 'in relation to an agency means any person who is registered as the provider or the manager of the agency'.

Service User Anyone who receives care or practical services from the local authority, a voluntary or independent agency, a housing or health service, or from self-employed or directly-employed home care workers. It also includes those 'informal' or 'family' carers who receive services in their own right under the Carers and Disabled Children Act 2000, or who employ a person to undertake tasks in their home in order that they can carry out their caring role.

Social Care Institute of Excellence (SCIE) A body which aims to improve the quality of social care. It will create a knowledge base of good practice in social care by sharing information on what works well, and produce good practice guidelines.

Social Security Office A generic term used to cover all offices which handle and process social security benefits claims. Until recently they were called Benefits Agency Offices, but they have been replaced with Job-Centre Plus for people of working age, the Pension Service for older people, and the Disability and Carers Benefit Service. Benefits Agency Offices are to be replaced gradually over the next few years.

Appendix 1
National Minimum Standards

The following extracts, taken from the **Domiciliary Care National Minimum Standards**, are those relevant to handling service users' money and belongings, and related issues such as confidentiality and record keeping. Those marked with an asterisk (*) also apply to employment agencies solely introducing workers.

Standard 5 Confidentiality

* 5.1 Care and support staff respect information given by service users or their representatives in confidence and handle information about service users in accordance with the Data Protection Act 1998 and the agency's written policies and procedures and in the best interests of the service user.

5.2 Service users have summaries of the agency's policies and procedures on confidentiality which specifies the circumstances under which confidentiality may be breached and includes the process for dealing with inappropriate breaches of confidentiality.

5.3 Care or support workers know when information given them in confidence must be shared with their manager and other social/health care agencies.

* 5.4 The principles of confidentiality are observed in discussion with colleagues and line manager, particularly when undertaking training or group supervision sessions.

* 5.5 Suitable provision is made for the safe and confidential storage of service user records and information including the provision of lockable filing cabinets and the shielding of computer screens from general view when displaying personal data.

Standard 9 Autonomy and independence

* 9.1 Managers and care and support workers enable service users to

make decisions in relation to their own lives, providing information, assistance, and support where needed.

* 9.2 Service users are encouraged, enabled and empowered to control their personal finances unless prevented from doing so by severe mental incapacity or disability.

* 9.3 Care and support workers carry out tasks *with* the service user, not *for* them, minimising the intervention and supporting service users to take risks, as set out in the service user plan and not endangering health and safety.

* 9.8 Limitations on the chosen lifestyle or human rights to prevent self-harm or self-neglect, or abuse or harm to others, are made only in the service user's best interest, consistent with the agency's responsibilities in law. The limitations are recorded in full within the risk assessment and the plan for managing the risks and entered into the service user plan.

Standard 13 Financial protection

13.1 The registered person ensures that there is a policy and there are procedures in place for staff on the safe handling of service users' money and property covering:

- payment for the service/service user's contribution (if appropriate)
- payment of bills
- shopping
- collection of pensions
- safeguarding the property of service users whilst undertaking the care tasks
- reporting the loss or damage to property whilst providing the care

and guidance on NOT:

- accepting gifts or cash (beyond a *very* minimal value)
- using loyalty cards except those belonging to the service user
- making personal use of the service user's property eg telephone
- involving the service user in gambling syndicates (eg national lottery, football pools)
- borrowing or lending of money

- selling or disposing of goods belonging to the service user and their family
- selling goods or services to the service user
- incurring a liability on behalf of the service user
- taking responsibility for looking after any valuables on behalf of the service user
- taking any unauthorised person (including children) or pets into the service user's home without permission of the service user, their relatives or representative and the manager of the service.

13.2 The agency's policies and practices regarding service users' wills and bequests preclude the involvement of any staff or members of their family, in the making of or benefiting from service users' wills or soliciting any other form of bequest or legacy or acting as witness or executor or being involved in any way with any other legal document.

13.3 The registered person ensures there is a policy and procedure for the investigation of allegations of financial irregularities and the involvement of police, social services and professional bodies.

13.4 The amount and purpose of all financial transactions undertaken on behalf of the services user, including shopping and the collection of pensions is recorded appropriately on the visit record held in the service user's home and signed and dated by the care and support worker and by the service user, if able to do so, or their relatives or representatives on their behalf.

13.5 Where services users are unable to take responsibility for the management of their own finances, this is recorded on the risk assessment and action taken to minimise the risk.

13.6 The registered person will keep a register that is open to inspection and owners and managers will declare in writing in the register any interest or involvement with any other separate organisation providing care or support services or responsible for commissioning or contracting those services, including where partners or other close family members own or manage at a senior level, other businesses providing domiciliary, day, residential or nursing care.

Standard 14 Protection of the person

14.1 Service users are safeguarded from any form of abuse or exploitation including physical, financial, psychological, sexual abuse, neglect, discriminatory abuse or self-harm or inhuman or degrading treatment through deliberate intent, negligence or ignorance in accordance with written policies and procedures.

14.2 The Registered Person ensures that the agency has robust procedures for responding to suspicion or evidence of abuse or neglect (including whistle blowing) to ensure the safety and protection of service users. The procedures reflect local multi-agency policies and procedures including the involvement of the Police and the passing on concerns to the NCSC in accordance with the Public Interest Disclosure Act 1998 and the Department of Health guidance *No Secrets*.

14.3 All allegations and incidents of abuse are followed up promptly and the details and action taken recorded in a special record/file kept for the purpose and on the personal file of the service user.

14.7 Training on prevention of abuse is given to all staff within 6 months of employment and is updated every two years.

Standard 15 Security of the home

15.1 Care and support workers ensure the security and safety of the home and the service user at all times when providing personal care.

15.2 Clear protocols are in place in relation to entering the homes of service users which cover:

- knocking/ringing bell and speaking out before entry
- written and signed agreements on keyholding
- safe handling and storage of keys outside the home
- confidentiality of entry codes
- alternative arrangements for entering the home
- action to take in case of loss or theft of keys
- action to take when unable to gain entry
- securing doors and windows
- discovery of an accident to the service user
- other emergency situations.

15.3 Identity cards are provided for all care and support staff entering the home of service users. The card should display:

- a photograph of the member of staff
- the name of the person and employing organisation in large print
- the contact number of the organisation
- date of issue and an expiry date which should not exceed 36 months from the date of issue.

The cards should be:

- available in large print for people with visual disabilities
- laminated or otherwise tamper proof
- renewed and replaced within at least 36 months from the date of issue
- returned to the organisation when employment ceases.

15.4 For people with special communication requirements, there are clear and agreed ways of identifying care and support staff from the agency.

Standard 16 Records kept in the home

16.1 With the user's consent, care or support workers record on records kept in the home of service users, the time and date of every visit to the home, the service provided and any significant occurrence. Where employed by *the agency*, live-in care and support workers complete the record on a daily basis. Records include (where appropriate):

- assistance with medication including time and dosage on a special medication chart
- other requests for assistance with medication and action taken
- financial transactions undertaken on behalf of the service user
- details of any changes in the user's or carer's circumstances, health, physical condition, care needs
- any accident, however minor, to the service user and/or care or support worker
- any other untoward incidents
- any other information which would assist the next health or social care worker to ensure consistency in the provisions of care.

16.2 Service users and/or their relatives or representatives are informed about what is written on the record and have access to it.

16.3 All written records are legible, factual, signed and dated and kept in a safe place in the home, as agreed with the service user, their relatives or representative.

16.4 Records are kept in the home for one month, or until the service is concluded, after which time they are transferred, with the permission of the service user, to the provider agency or other suitable body (eg local authority or health trust, or other purchaser of the service), for safe keeping.

16.5 Any service user or their relatives or representative on their behalf, refusing to have records kept in their home, is requested to sign and date a statement confirming the refusal and this is kept on their personal file in the agency.

Standard 23 Financial procedures

* 23.1 The registered person ensures that sound accounting and other financial procedures are adopted to ensure the effective and efficient running of the business and its continued financial viability.

* 23.2 Systems are in place so that accurate calculation can be made of the charges for the service, to submit invoices regularly and to identify and follow-up any late payment.

* 23.4 Insurance cover is sufficient to protect the agency's assets and liabilities. Including the agency's legal liabilities to any and all employees and third party persons to a limit of indemnity commensurate with the level and extent of activities undertaken.

Standard 24 Record keeping

* 24.1 The agency maintains all the records required for the protection of service users and the efficient running of the business for the requisite length of time including:

- financial records detailing all transactions *
- personal file on each service user
- personnel files on each member of staff *

- interview of applicants for posts who are subsequently employed *
- accident report record
- record of incidents of abuse or suspected abuse (including use of restraint) and action taken *
- record of complaints and compliments and action taken *
- records of disciplinary and grievance procedures *
- records kept in the home of service users.

* 24.2 All records are secure, up to date and in good order and are constructed, maintained and used in accordance with the Data Protection Act 1998, and other statutory requirements and are kept for the requisite length of time.

24.3 Consistent and standard personal data is kept on all service users being cared for by the agency, except for employment agencies solely introducing workers.

24.4 Service users or their representatives have access to their records and information about them held by the agency and are facilitated in obtaining access when necessary.

Standard 25 Policies and procedures

* 25.1 The agency implements a clear set of policies and procedures to support practice and meet the requirements of legislation, which are dated, and monitored, as part of the quality assurance process. The policies and procedures are reviewed and amended annually or more frequently if necessary.

* 25.2 Staff understand and have access to up-to-date copies of all policies, procedures and codes of practice and service users have access to relevant information on the policies and procedures and other documents in appropriate formats.

Crown copyright material is reproduced with the permission of the Controller of HMSO and the Queen's Printer for Scotland.

Appendix 2
Local Government Ombudsman cases on gifts and wills

The following summaries are some of the Local Government Ombudsman cases relating to gifts and wills.

94/C/4417 Against Stockport MBC

The complaint was that an employee wrongly accepted a legacy and might have wrongly accepted money from a service user, and might also have sought to influence the will. There was a period when the home care worker visited as a friend when the service user was in a privately run home. The family complained about financial loss.

The Ombudsman found that the Council had failed to make clear when a person ceased to be a client (the home care worker had visited as a friend), that the home care worker would have been well advised to seek advice from her manager about whether to accept the legacy. Accepting the legacy was maladministration, but this was because the Council had failed to make matters clear. The Ombudsman stated it was for the courts to decide whether undue influence had occurred so as to invalidate the will. Although in this case, on the facts presented, the Ombudsman did not consider it was reasonable to ask the Council to pay back the money relating to the lost inheritance, it was felt the complaint was justified and recommended the payment of £300 to the family for the time and trouble in making the complaint.

96/C/2660 Against North Yorkshire CC

The complaint concerned a bequest to a home care worker, who had also worked privately for a service user. The local authority had procedures on gifts, bequests and conflict of interest, which were given on employment, although the home care workers were not asked to sign for them. A new conflict of interest policy was produced and distributed to staff in their pay slips and discussed at team meetings. The home care worker later denied knowledge of the new policy. In 1994, the service user made his will and left a five figure sum to his home care worker, who was told that she was a beneficiary. Part of the complaint was that the home care worker had discussed the making of a will with the service user. The home care worker notified the local authority of the inheritance several months after the service user died and a senior officer investigated the bequest. The home care worker was told that, subject to agreement from the Director of Social Services, no disciplinary action would be taken as she had not exercised undue influence. Only the home care worker was interviewed. The investigation was deferred when a complaint was received from the family. Although the home care worker was able to keep the bequest, there was a disciplinary hearing.

Following the complaint, the Council decided to change its policies and procedures. Workers were instructed not to enter into any discussions about wills with clients. A new code of conduct about investigating bequests was also produced, as was a new leaflet for service users, placing greater emphasis on the issue of gifts and bequests. The Council has also changed its policy so staff now have to sign for receipt of the guidance. In view of this, and a promise to pay the family £600, the complaint was discontinued.

99/B/1651 Against Suffolk CC

A home care worker provided care over a number of years to a service user who, in 1986, made a will leaving money to the home care worker. In 1991, the service user also made a payment of £1,000 and made another will, leaving one sixth of her estate to the home care worker. In 1993, the home care worker was left a dog under another service user's will, together with money to care for it. Following this, the home care worker received written confirmation of the restrictions on receiving legacies, that it was not the responsibility of home care workers to help clients with financial matters and that it was unprofessional to discuss their own finances with them or make unscheduled visits. She was given a new post in a different part of the county and ceased to be the home care worker of the service user. She did not advise the Council of the gift of £1,000 in 1991, in spite of now having the policy on gifts and legacies. The Council was aware that the home care worker still visited the client as a friend. The family was concerned that the home care worker was purchasing alcohol for the client against their wishes. The client moved to residential care.

The family took on the power of attorney and wrote to the Council in 1996 regarding the £1,000 and the legacy to the home care worker. No investigation was undertaken. Following an incident at the residential home with the home care worker and the service user, the family expressed further concerns after a case conference and the officer advised the family to write to the Council. A letter was sent in 1998. It was not until 1999, after the service user's death, that an investigation started and only the home care worker was interviewed. The family complained about the delay in the investigation.

The Ombudsman found many unsatisfactory aspects to the events. The Council's expectation of its staff were laid down in 1984 and by Director's instruction in 1990. However, they cannot confirm that staff received it as there was no signature required to record this. This was maladministration. The home care worker admitted knowing about a rule of £5 gifts but failed to declare a gift of £1,000. This was maladministration. In 1996, when the Council received a letter from the family complaining about providing alcohol, the £1,000 gift and the legacy, matters were not followed up. These failings were 'lamentable' and were maladministration. In 1998, when the complaint was revived, there was still no investigation, and no investigation started until after the death of the service user, three years after the concerns were first raised. This was further maladministration. The investigation that was carried out was 'woefully inadequate', with no evidence being sought from third parties, and no consideration appeared to have been given to enforce the Council's policy that in no circumstances should a gift of money be accepted, or that it should be paid into a welfare fund if it could not be refused without giving offence. This was also maladministration. An ex gratia payment of £2,000 was recommended by the

Ombudsman, together with an urgent review of the Council's arrangements for requiring standards of conduct of its care staff, for communicating those requirements and for specifying what action will be taken when infringements are discovered.

See Appendix 4 for contact details of the Local Government Ombudsmen.

Appendix 3
Further reading

Action on Elder Abuse (2000). *The home front.* AEA. (Video training package).

Action on Elder Abuse (1997). *The abuse of older people at home.* AEA.

Age Concern England (1999). *Home and personal safety: Resource Pack 23.* Services Development, Research and Development Unit, ACE.

Age Concern England (2001). *Confronting elder abuse: policies and procedures in Age Concern.* Research and Development Unit, ACE.

Bell, L. (1999). *CareFully: a handbook for home care assistants (2nd edition).* Age Concern Books.

Bell, L. (1996). *Managing careFully: a guide for home care managers.* Age Concern Books.

British Association of Domiciliary Care Officers. *Handling service users' finances and valuables.* BADCO.

Department of Health (DH) (2002). *Domiciliary care: national minimum standards.* London.

DH (2002). *Keep warm, keep well.* London. (Updated annually)

DH (2000). *No Secrets: guidance on developing and implementing multi-agency policies and procedures to protect vulnerable adults from abuse.* London.

DH (2001 and 2002). *Fairer charging policies for home care and other non-residential services.* London.

Disability Alliance (2002). *Charges for community care services: a guide for disabled people and carers in England and Wales.* Disability Alliance. (Also available on audio tape)

Disability Alliance (2002). *Disability rights handbook 2002–2003 (27th Edition)*. Disability Alliance. (Updated annually)

Disablement Income Group (2002). *Recruiting and employing a care worker*. DIG.

Inland Revenue. *Employed or self-employed? A guide for tax and national insurance*. (Ref: IR56/N139).

Letts, P. (1998). *Managing other people's money*. Age Concern Books.

National Centre for Independent Living (2000). *The rough guide to managing personal assistants*. NCIL.

Pritchard, J. (1999). *Elder abuse work: best practice in Britain and Canada*. Jessica Kingsley Publishers.

Pritchard, J. (1995). *The abuse of older people: a training manual for detection and prevention*. Jessica Kingsley Publishers.

Slater, E. and Eastman, M. (eds.) (1999). *Elder abuse: critical issues in policy and practice*. Age Concern Books.

Tait, G. et al. (2002). *Paying for care handbook (3rd Edition)*. Child Poverty Action Group. (Updated annually)

United Kingdom Home Care Association. *Managing finance: UKHCA guidelines*. UKHCA.

West, S. (2002). *Your Rights 2002–2003: a guide to money benefits for older people*. Age Concern Books. (Updated annually)

Appendix 4
Useful contacts

Action on Elder Abuse (AEA)
Astral House, 1268 London Road
London SW16 4ER
Tel: 020 8765 7000
Fax: 020 8679 4074
Helpline: 080 8808 8141 (Freephone, Mon–Fri, 10am–4.30pm)
Email: aea@ace.org.uk
Website: www.elderabuse.org.uk

Age Concern Information Line (ACIL)
FREEPOST (SWB 30375)
Ashburton, Devon TQ13 7ZZ
Tel: 0800 00 99 66 (Freephone)
Provides Factsheets and Information sheets referenced in the book. There is also a Factsheet subscription service (see page 164).

Age Concern Training (ACT)
Martindale, Hawks Green Lane
Hawks Green, Cannock
Staffordshire WS11 2XN
Tel: 01543 503660
Fax: 01543 504640
Website: www.ageconcern.org.uk
Provides care and management skills training, including 'elder abuse' and 'abuse of vulnerable adults'.

Alzheimer's Society
Gordon House, 10 Greencoat Place
London SW1P 1PH
Tel: 020 7306 0606
Helpline: 0845 300 0336
Fax: 020 7306 0808

Email: info@alzheimers.org.uk
Website: www.alzheimers.org.uk

Benefits Enquiry Line
Tel: 0800 88 22 00 (Freephone)

British Association Domiciliary Care Officers (BADCO)
6 Meadow View, Winnersh
Wokingham
Berkshire RG41 5PD
Tel/fax: 0118 977 2878
Website: www.badco.org

British Bankers' Association (BBA)
105–108 Old Broad Street
London EC2N 1EX
Tel: 020 7216 8800
Fax: 020 7216 8811
Website: www.bba.org.uk

Care and Repair England
Bridgford House
Pavilion Road
West Bridgford
Nottingham NG2 5GJ
Tel: 0115 982 1527
Fax: 0115 982 1529
Email: careandrepair@freenetname.co.uk
Website: www.careandrepair-england.org.uk

Carers UK
20–25 Glasshouse Yard
London EC1A 4JT
Tel: 020 7490 8818
Tel: 0808 808 7777 (Carers advice line)
Fax: 020 7490 8824
Email: info@ukcarers.org
Website: www.carersonline.org.uk

Child Poverty Action Group (CPAG)
94 White Lion Street
London N1 9PF
Tel: 020 7837 7979
Fax: 020 7837 6414
Email: staff@cpag.demon.co.uk
Website: www.cpag.org.uk

Coalition on Charging
c/o Disability Alliance
Universal House
88–94 Wentworth Street
London E1 7SA
Tel: 020 7247 8776 (Voice and textphone)
Fax: 020 7247 8765
Email: coalitiononcharging@mencap.org.uk
Website: www.mencap.org.uk/coc

Counsel and Care
Twyman House
16 Bonny Street
London NW1 9PG
Tel: 020 7241 8555 (Administration)
Advice Line: 0845 300 7585 (10am–1pm)
Fax: 020 7267 6877
Email: advice@counselandcare.org.uk
Website: www.counselandcare.org.uk
Offers free counselling, information and advice for older people and carers.

Department of Health (DH)
PO Box 777
London SE1 6XH
Tel: 08701 555455 (Publications)
Fax: 01623 724524
Email: doh@prolog.uk.com
Website: www.doh.gov.uk

DIAL UK
Park Lodge, St Catherine's Hospital
Tickhill Road, Doncaster
South Yorkshire DN4 8QN
Tel: 01302 310123 (Disability information)
Fax: 01302 310 404
Email: dialuk@aol.com
*DIAL UK is the national organisation for the DIAL (Disablement
Information and Advice Lines) network.*

Disability Alliance
Universal House
88–94 Wentworth Street
London E1 7SA
Tel: 020 7247 8776 (Voice and textphone)
Fax: 020 7247 8765
Email: office.da@dial.pipex.com
Website: www.disabilityalliance.org

The Disablement Income Group (DIG)
PO Box 5743
Finchingfield CM7 4PW
Tel: 01371 811621
Fax: 01371 811633

Eaga Ltd
Eldon Square
Newcastle upon Tyne NE1 7HA
Tel: 0800 181667 (Freephone)
Advice on insulation and Warm Front Grants.

Financial Services Authority (FSA)
25 The North Colonnade
Canary Wharf
London E14 5HS
Consumer helpline: 0845 606 1234
Email: consumerhelp@fsa.gov.uk
Website: www.fsa.gov.uk

Foundations
Bleaklow House, Howard Town Mills
Glossop, Derbyshire SK13 8HT
Tel: 01457 891909
Fax: 01457 869361
Email: foundations@cel.co.uk
Website: www.foundations.uk.com
The national co-ordinating body for Home Improvement Agencies (HIAs).

General Social Care Council (GSCC)
Goldings House, 2 Hays Lane
London SE1 2HB
Tel: 020 7397 5100
Email: info@gscc.org.uk
Website: www.doh.gov.uk/gscc

Help the Aged
207–221 Pentonville Road
London N1 9UZ
Tel: 020 7278 1114
Textphone: 0800 26 96 26
Seniorline: 0808 800 6565
Fax: 020 7278 1116
Email: info@helptheaged.org.uk
Website: www.helptheaged.org.uk

Independent Living Fund (ILF)
PO Box 7525
Nottingham NG2 4ZT
Tel: 0845 601 8815
Fax: 0115 929 6022
Email: funds@ilf.org.uk
Website: www.ilf.org.uk

Inland Revenue Enquiry Centres
Tel: 020 7667 4001 (General helpline, Mon–Fri, 8.30am–5pm)
Website: www.inlandrevenue.gov.uk
Check Yellow Pages or the website for your local centre, or contact the helpline for information.

Local Government Ombudsman (1)
21 Queen Anne's Gate
London SW1H 9BU
Tel: 020 7915 3210
Fax: 020 7233 0396
Website: www.lgo.org.uk
Covers London boroughs north of the river Thames (including Richmond but not including Harrow or Tower Hamlets), Essex, Kent, Surrey, Suffolk, East and West Sussex, Berkshire, Buckinghamshire, Hertfordshire and the City of Coventry.

Local Government Ombudsman (2)
Beverley House
17 Shipton Road
York YO30 5FZ
Tel: 01904 663200
Fax: 01904 663269
Website: www.lgo.org.uk
Covers London Borough of Tower Hamlets, City of Birmingham, Cheshire, Derbyshire, Nottinghamshire, Lincolnshire and the north of England (except the Cities of York and Lancaster).

Local Government Ombudsman (3)
The Oaks No 2
Westwood Way
Westwood Business Park
Coventry CV4 8JB
Tel: 024 7669 5999
Fax: 024 7669 5902
Website: www.lgo.org.uk
Covers London boroughs south of the river Thames (except Richmond) and Harrow; the Cities of York and Lancaster; and the rest of England, not included in the areas outlined in (1) and (2) above.

Mail Preference Service
Freepost 22
London W1E 7EZ
Helps service users to avoid unwanted post.

MIND
Granta House, 15–19 The Broadway
London E15 4BQ
Tel: 020 8519 2122
Tel: 020 8522 1728 (London information line)
Tel: 0845 766 0163 (Outside London information line)
Website: www.mind.org.uk

National Care Standards Commission (NCSC)
St Nicholas Building, St Nicholas Street
Newcastle upon Tyne NE1 1NB
Tel: 0191 233 3600
Website: www.carestandards.org.uk

National Centre for Independent Living (NCIL)
250 Kennington Lane
London SE11 5RD
Tel: 020 7587 1663
Email: ncil@ncil.org.uk
Website: www.ncil.org.uk

Pensions and Overseas Benefits Directorate
Tyneview Park, Whitley Road
Benton, Newcastle upon Tyne NE98 1BA
Tel: 0191 218 7878

Public Concern at Work
Suite 306, 16 Baldwins Gardens
London EC1N 7RJ
Tel: 020 7404 6609 (General enquiries and helpline)
Fax: 020 7407 6576
Emails: whistle@pcaw.co.uk (UK enquiries); helpline@pcaw.co.uk
(UK helpline); services@pcaw.co.uk (UK services)

Public Guardianship Office
Archway Tower
2 Junction Road
London N19 5SZ
Tel: 0845 330 2900 (Customer services)

Textphone: 020 7664 7755
Fax: 020 7664 7705 (Customer services)
Email: custserv@guardianship.gov.uk
Website: www.guardianship.gov.uk

The Royal British Legion
48 Pall Mall
London SW1Y 5JY
Tel: 020 7973 7200
Fax: 020 7973 7399
Email: info@britishlegion.org.uk
Website: www.britishlegion.org.uk

Royal National Institute for Deaf People (RNID)
19–23 Featherstone Street
London EC1Y 8SL
Helpline: 0808 808 0123
Textphone: 0808 808 9000
Website: www.rnid.org.uk

Royal National Institute of the Blind (RNIB)
105 Judd Street
London WC1H 9NE
Tel: 020 7388 1266
Helpline: 0845 766 99 99 (Mon–Fri, 9am to 5pm)
Fax: 020 7388 2034
Email: rnib@rnib.org.uk
Website: www.rnib.org.uk

Social Care Institute for Excellence (SCIE)
1st Floor, Goldings House
2 Hay's Lane
London SE1 2HB
Tel: 020 7089 6840
Website: www.scie.org.uk

Staying Put
Tel: 08457 75 85 95 (Customer enquiries, Mon–Fri, 9am–5pm)
Email: enquiries@anchor.org.uk
Website: www.anchor.org.uk
Anchor Staying Put helps older and disabled homeowners to repair and improve their properties so they can 'stay put' and retain their independence.

Telephone Preference Service
Tel: 0845 0700 707
Helps service users to avoid unwanted calls.

United Kingdom Home Care Association (UKHCA)
42b Banstead Road
Carshalton Beeches
Surrey SM5 3NW
Tel: 020 8288 1551
Fax: 020 8288 1550
Email: enquiries@ukhca.demon.co.uk
Website: www.ukhca.co.uk

Veterans Agency
Norcross
Blackpool FY5 3WP
Helpline: 0800 169 2277 (Freephone)
Previously the War Pensions Agency.

Victim Support
Cranmer House
39 Brixton Road
London SW9 6DZ
Tel: 020 7735 9166
Helpline: 0845 303 0900

Warm Front Grants
Tel: 0800 316 6011 (Freephone)

About Age Concern

Money at Home is one of a wide range of publications produced by Age Concern England, the National Council on Ageing. Age Concern works on behalf of all older people and believes later life should be fulfilling and enjoyable. For too many, this is impossible. As the leading charitable movement in the UK concerned with ageing and older people, Age Concern finds effective ways to change that situation.

Where possible, we enable older people to solve problems themselves, providing as much or as little support as they need. Locally, Age Concern provides community-based services such as lunch clubs, day centres and home visiting. These services are made possible through the work of many thousands of volunteers.

Nationally, we take a lead role in campaigning, parliamentary work, policy analysis, research, specialist information and advice provision, and publishing. Innovative programmes promote healthier lifestyles and provide older people with opportunities to give the experience of a lifetime back to their communities.

Age Concern is dependent on donations, covenants and legacies.

Age Concern England
1268 London Road
London SW16 4ER
Tel: 020 8765 7200
Fax: 020 8765 7211

Age Concern Scotland
113 Rose Street
Edinburgh EH2 3DT
Tel: 0131 220 3345
Fax: 0131 220 2779

Age Concern Cymru
4th Floor, 1 Cathedral Road
Cardiff CF11 9SD
Tel: 029 2037 1566
Fax: 029 2039 9562

Age Concern Northern Ireland
3 Lower Crescent
Belfast BT7 1NR
Tel: 028 9024 5729
Fax: 028 9023 5497

Publications from
Age Concern Books

CareFully: A handbook for home care assistants (2nd edition)
Lesley Bell

Covering all of the key issues concerning the Care Standards Act 2000 and the regulation of domiciliary care, and complete with case studies and checklists, this is a book to enable all home care workers to face their job with confidence and enthusiasm.

£12.99   0-86242-285-X

Managing CareFully: A guide for managers of home care services
Lesley Bell

This handbook provides advice and guidance for managers of home care services in the private, voluntary and local authority sectors. It supplies detailed background information on the community care reforms and service provision, and explores in full:

- assessment of local needs
- legal requirements
- selecting staff
- handling clients' money
- complaints
- managing standards
- business planning
- responding to clients' changing needs.

The contents of each chapter are related to the relevant NVQ 4 and NVQ 5 Management Standards.

£14.99   0-86242-185-3

Elder Abuse: Critical issues in policy and practice
Edited by Phil Slater and Mervyn Eastman

Written primarily for anyone working in the areas of health and social care – as well as for relevant academics – this book provides a sound framework to explore good practice and to support the recognition, management and prevention of elder abuse. The contributing authors are drawn evenly from the worlds of service provision and academic research and they explore:

- models of understanding and intervention
- elder abuse and social work
- challenges to professional education
- promoting user participation
- lessons from research
- international considerations
- developing policies and procedures
- elder abuse in care home settings.

£14.99   0-86242-248-5

An Introductory Guide to Community Care
Alan Goodenough

This book is a useful starting point for new or inexperienced carers, particularly paid carers, who are unsure of what services are available or who they can turn to for support or advice. It guides them through the basics of care plans, relevant legislation and regulations, useful contacts, and the roles of other professionals they will encounter. The book encourages the carer to feel part of a team, offers self-assessment opportunities, and encourages them to seek further training opportunities.

£6.99   0-86242-340-6

Staying Sane: Managing the stress of caring
Tanya Arroba and Lesley Bell

There is no doubt that providing care to people in their own homes can be very rewarding work – and at the same time very demanding. The demands on the carer are many and can become overwhelming if not managed. The aim of this book is to increase the positive rewards associated with caring and demystify the topic of stress. In particular, this book will:

- increase awareness and understanding of stress
- encourage awareness of the importance of dealing with stress as a carer

- identify and explore the pressures and demands involved in caring
- outline approaches for maintaining mental and emotional balance as a carer.

Complete with case studies and checklists, this is a book to help and support all carers in developing a clear strategy towards dealing positively with stress and staying sane.

£14.99   0-86242-267-1

Residents' Money: A guide to good practice in care homes

This guide is for people who work in residential and nursing homes who may be involved in handling residents' money or in helping them to manage their financial affairs. It includes detailed advice for care managers and staff on how to design and put into practice policies that reflect the very best in good practice.

£7.99   0-86242-205-1

Managing Other People's Money (2nd edition)
Penny Letts

Ideal for both the family carer and for legal and other advice workers, this new edition is essential reading for anyone facing this challenging situation. Providing a step-by-step guide to the arrangements which have to be made, topics include:

- when to take over
- the powers available
- enduring power of attorney
- Court of Protection
- claiming benefits
- collecting pensions and salaries
- living arrangements
- residential care.

£9.99   0-86242-250-7

Please note this book does not cover legal arrangements in Scotland or Northern Ireland

If you would like to order any of these titles, please write to the address below, enclosing a cheque or money order for the appropriate amount (plus £1.95 p&p) made payable to Age Concern England. Credit card orders may be made on 0870 44 22 044 (for individuals); or 0870 44 22 120 (Age Concerns, other organisations and institutions). Fax: 0870 44 22 034.

Age Concern Books
PO Box 232
Newton Abbot
Devon TQ12 4XQ

Age Concern Information Line/Factsheets subscription

Age Concern produces more than 40 comprehensive factsheets designed to answer many of the questions older people (or those advising them) may have. Topics covered include money and benefits, health, community care, leisure and education, and housing. For up to five free factsheets, telephone: 0800 00 99 66 (7am–7pm, seven days a week, every day of the year). Alternatively you may prefer to write to Age Concern, FREEPOST (SWB 30375), Ashburton, Devon TQ13 7ZZ.

For professionals working with older people, the factsheets are available on an annual subscription service, which includes updates throughout the year. For further details and costs of the subscription, write to Age Concern at the above Freepost address.

Index